Ecce Romani

A Latin Reading Program
Revised Edition

1
Meeting the Family

Ecce Romani Student's Book 1   Meeting the Family

First Printing 1984

ISBN 0 582 36664 X
(72458)

Illustrated by Peter Dennis, Trevor Parkin, and Hamish Gordon. Cover illustration by Peter Dennis.

This edition of *Ecce Romani* is based on *Ecce Romani: A Latin Reading Course*, originally prepared by The Scottish Classics Group © copyright The Scottish Classics Group 1971, 1982, and published in the United Kingdom by Oliver and Boyd, a Division of Longman Group. This edition has been prepared by a team of American and Canadian educators:

  Authors: Professor Gilbert Lawall, University of Massachusetts, Amherst, Massachusetts

           David Tafe, Rye Country Day School, Rye, New York

  Consultants: Dr. Rudolph Masciantonio, Philadelphia Public Schools, Pennsylvania

           Ronald Palma, Holland Hall School, Tulsa, Oklahoma

           Dr. Edward Barnes, C.W. Jefferys Secondary School, Downsview, Ontario

           Shirley Lowe, Wayland Public Schools, Wayland, Massachusetts

Longman, 10 Bank Street, White Plains, N.Y. 10606

Distributed in Canada by Academic Press Ltd., 55 Barber Greene Road, Don Mills, Ontario MC3 2A1, Canada.

13 14 15 16 17 18 19 20-CRW-9998979695

CONTENTS

1
Two Roman Girls

Ecce! In pictūrā est puella, nōmine Cornēlia. Cornēlia est puella Rōmāna quae in Italiā habitat. Etiam in pictūrā est vīlla rūstica ubi Cornēlia aestāte habitat. Cornēlia est laeta quod iam in vīllā habitat. Cornēlia iam sub arbore sedet. Etiam in pictūrā est altera puella, nōmine Flāvia. Flāvia est puella Rōmāna quae in vīllā vīcīnā habitat. Dum Cornēlia sedet, Flāvia cantat. 5
Laeta est Flāvia quod Cornēlia iam in vīllā habitat.

Ecce! Look!
puella, (a, the) girl
nōmine, by name, called
quae, who
habitat, (he, she) is living, lives
etiam, also
ubi, where
aestāte, in summer
laeta, happy

quod, because
iam, now
sub arbore, under the tree
sedet, (he, she) is sitting, sits
altera, a second
vīcīna, neighboring
dum, while
cantat, (he, she) is singing, sings

Exercise 1a

Respondē Latīnē:
1. Quis est Cornēlia?
2. Ubi habitat Cornēlia?
3. Cūr est Cornēlia laeta?
4. Quid facit Cornēlia?

5. Ubi habitat Flāvia?
6. Quid facit Flāvia?
7. Cūr est Flāvia laeta?

Quis . . . ? Who . . . ?

Cūr . . . ? Why . . . ?
Quid facit . . . ? What does . . . do?
What is . . . doing?

Exercise 1b

From the passage give the Latin for:
1. Cornelia is happy.
2. Cornelia is sitting under the tree.
3. Flavia is a Roman girl.
4. Cornelia now lives in the farmhouse.

2
A Happy Outing

Cornēlia est puella Rōmāna. Flāvia quoque est puella Rōmāna. Cornēlia et Flāvia sunt puellae Rōmānae quae in Italiā habitant. Cornēlia et Flāvia sunt amīcae. Hodiē puellae nōn sedent sed in agrīs ambulant. Puellae cantant quod laetae sunt. Brevī tempore Cornēlia dēfessa est. Nōn iam ambulat sed sub arbore sedet. Flāvia, quae est puella strēnua, in agrīs currit. Brevī tempore 5 Flāvia quoque est dēfessa. Iam Flāvia et Cornēlia sub arbore sedent quod dēfessae sunt. Tandem puellae dēfessae ex agrīs ad vīllam rūsticam lentē ambulant.

quoque, also
et, and
sunt, (they) are
amīcae, friends
hodiē, today
sed, but
in agrīs, in the fields
ambulant, (they) are walking, walk
brevī tempore, in a short time, soon

dēfessa, tired
strēnua, active, energetic
currit, (he, she) is running, runs
tandem, at last
ex agrīs, from the fields
ad vīllam rūsticam, to or toward the farmhouse
lentē, slowly

VERBS: The Endings -t and -nt

Look at these sentences:

Flāvia in Italiā habitat.   *Flavia lives in Italy.*
Puella in agrīs currit.   *The girl is running in the fields.*
Flāvia et Cornēlia in Italiā habitant.   *Flavia and Cornelia live in Italy.*
Puellae sub arbore sedent.   *The girls are sitting under the tree.*

When the verb ends in -t, the subject of the sentence is singular, e.g., **Flāvia, puella.**

When the verb ends in -nt, the subject of the sentence is plural, e.g., **Flāvia et Cornēlia, puellae.**

6

Exercise 2a

Respondē Latīnē:
1. Ubi habitant Cornēlia et Flāvia?
2. Quid faciunt puellae hodiē? **Quid faciunt . . . ?**
   What are . . . doing?
3. Cūr puellae cantant?
4. Quid facit Cornēlia quod dēfessa est?
5. Quid faciunt puellae quod dēfessae sunt?

Exercise 2b

From the passage give the Latin for:
1. Cornelia and Flavia are Roman girls.
2. In a short time Cornelia is tired.
3. Flavia is running in the fields.
4. At last the girls walk slowly to the farmhouse.

Exercise 2c

Select the correct word, read the sentence aloud, and translate it into English:
1. Flāvia in vīllā vīcīnā _____. habitat / habitant
2. Cornēlia et Flāvia sub arbore _____. sedet / sedent
3. Cornēlia et Flāvia dēfessae _____. est / sunt
4. Flāvia strēnua _____. est / sunt
5. Cornēlia et Flāvia sunt _____. puella Rōmāna / puellae Rōmānae

Exercise 2d

Read aloud and translate:
Cornēlia est puella Rōmāna quae in vīllā rūsticā aestāte habitat. In vīllā vīcīnā habitat altera puella, nōmine Flāvia, quae est amīca eius. Dum puellae in vīllā habitant, in agrīs saepe ambulant. Hodiē Cornēlia ad vīllam Flāviānam ambulat ubi in agrīs sub arbore sedet Flāvia. Iam puellae laetae currunt. Brevī tempore, quod dēfessae sunt, 5 nōn iam currunt sed sub arbore sedent.

eius, her   **saepe,** often

7

A Roman Family

The stories and pictures in this book are about a Roman family. When we first meet them, they are living not in Rome but on a farm (**fundus**) in the country near Baiae in Campania.

While spending their summers on the farm, the family occupies part of a large farmhouse called a **vīlla** or **vīlla rūstica** which has a central farmyard, court, or garden (**hortus**) surrounded by living quarters for the owner's family in one corner, a second farmyard with wine vats sunk in the ground, and various farm buildings including rooms for the slave laborers.

The date is A.D. 80.

In our family, there is a daughter, Cornelia, who is thirteen, and a son, Marcus, fifteen. Both wear the same dress as their respective parents, Cornelius and Aurelia, because the Romans did not have special clothes for children. Neither goes to school when at the **vīlla,** their education being in the hands of a Greek tutor, Eucleides. Although the father is called Gaius Cornelius Calvus and the son Marcus Cornelius Calvus, the daughter has to be content with the feminine form of her father's name, Cornelia. (What must Aurelia's father have been called?) Although Marcus has lessons from Eucleides, he gets a good deal of his education directly from his father, for Gaius is an old-fashioned Roman who thinks a father should superintend his son's education personally.

Gaius is responsible for the estate. As father, he is not only master of his own house, but legally has the power of life and death over his entire household, though he never exercises this power. Aurelia runs the household. She does some wool-spinning—a traditional practice which recalls the old Roman ideal of self-sufficiency—but, unlike the modern housewife, she has a miniature army of slaves to help with the chores.

They have living with them a younger boy, Sextus. He is not related to the family, but Cornelius is acting as his guardian while his father is on service overseas. Also with the family, from time to time, is Cornelia's friend, Flavia, who lives in a neighboring farmhouse referred to as the **vīlla Flāviāna** because it is owned by her father, Flavius.

Most Roman families had slaves who did the everyday work of the household and the farms. The tutor, Eucleides, is a slave, as is Davus, the overseer of the slaves and the farm.

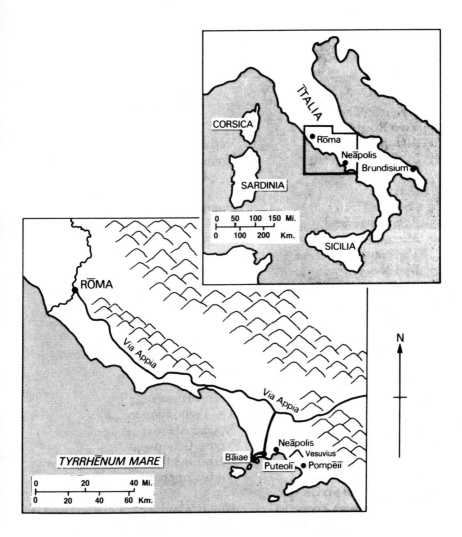

Baiae, on the Bay of Naples, was a fashionable resort for wealthy Romans, many of whom built splendid villas there. Puteoli, further around the Bay, was a thriving seaport where corn-ships from Egypt and Sicily would unload their cargo, to be taken to Rome by road. Nearby Naples (**Neāpolis**), a center of culture and learning for the Romans, was far enough from Vesuvius to survive when the eruption of A.D. 79 overwhelmed the prosperous town of Pompeii.

This whole area, part of the fertile province of Campania, in summer attracted Romans who were seeking relief from the heat and noise of Rome in this "Garden of Italy."

9

3
In the Garden

In pictūrā est puer Rōmānus, nōmine Marcus, quī in Italiā habitat. Etiam
in pictūrā est alter puer, nōmine Sextus, quī in eādem vīllā rūsticā habitat.
Marcus et Sextus sunt amīcī. Hodiē puerī in hortō clāmant et rīdent quod
laetī sunt.

Vir quoque est in pictūrā, nōmine Dāvus, quī est servus. In Italiā sunt 5
multī servī quī in agrīs et in vīllīs rūsticīs labōrant. Puerī sunt Rōmānī, sed
Dāvus nōn est Rōmānus. Est vir Britannicus quī iam in Italiā labōrat. Sextus
et Marcus, quod sunt puerī Rōmānī, nōn labōrant. Dāvus sōlus labōrat,
īrātus quod puerī clāmant.

Subitō Sextus in piscīnam cadit. Marcus rīdet, sed Dāvus, "Abīte, 10
molestī!" clāmat et ad piscīnam īrātus currit. Sextus madidus ex piscīnā
exit, et puerī ex hortō currunt. Dāvus gemit.

puer, (a, the) boy	**in vīllīs rūsticīs,** in farmhouses
quī, who	**labōrant,** (they) are working, work
eādem, the same	**sōlus,** alone
in hortō, in the garden	**īrātus,** angry
clāmant, (they) are shouting, shout	**subitō,** suddenly
rīdent, (they) are laughing, laugh, smile	**in piscīnam,** into the fishpond
vir, (a, the) man	**cadit,** (he, she) falls
servus, (a, the) slave	**Abīte, molestī!** Go away, you pests!
multī, many	**madidus,** dripping, soaked
	gemit, (he, she) groans

11

Exercise 3a

Respondē Latīnē:
1. Quis est Dāvus?
2. Estne Marcus servus?
3. Quis est Marcus?
4. Suntne Marcus et Sextus amīcī?
5. Quid faciunt puerī hodiē?
6. Cūr Dāvus īrātus est?
7. Estne Dāvus vir Rōmānus?
8. Quid subitō facit Sextus?

Estne . . . ? Is . . . ?

Minimē! No!
Ita vērō! Yes!

Exercise 3b

From the passage give the Latin for:
1. Today the boys laugh because they are happy.
2. In Italy there are many slaves who work in farmhouses.
3. Davus now works in Italy.
4. Davus runs to the fishpond, and the boys run out of the garden.

NOUNS: Singular and Plural

Note how these words change in the plural:

Singular	Plural
puella	puellae
servus	servī
puer	puerī

Compare also: puella Rōmāna   puellae Rōmānae
              puer Rōmānus   puerī Rōmānī

12

Exercise 3c

Select, read aloud, and translate:

1. Marcus et Sextus in eādem vīllā _____. habitat / habitant
2. Dāvus vir Britannicus _____. est / sunt
3. In agrīs labōrant _____. servus / servī
4. Puerī et puellae saepe _____. gemit / currit / currunt
5. In agrīs sunt multī _____. puella / servus / servī
6. In Italiā habitat _____. Marcus et Sextus/
   Marcus / puellae
7. Marcus et Sextus sunt puerī _____. Rōmānus / Rōmānī /
   Rōmānae
8. Cornēlia et Flāvia sunt puellae _____. Rōmānus / Rōmānī /
   Rōmānae

Exercise 3d

Read aloud and translate:

Hodiē Sextus in hortō ambulat sōlus quod Marcus in vīllā sedet.
Sextus est puer strēnuus quī saepe in agrīs et in hortō currit. Brevī
tempore Dāvus in hortum ambulat, sollicitus quod Sextus in hortō
est. Dum Dāvus labōrat, Sextus eum spectat. Sextus Dāvum saepe
vexat, sed hodiē nihil facit.   5
  In hortum ad piscīnam currunt Flāvia et Cornēlia. Laetae rīdent
et clāmant. Sextus fūrtim ad piscīnam ambulat. Subitō in piscīnam
cadit statua rūstica. Madidae iam sunt puellae et īrātae. Dāvus est
sollicitus quod statua est in piscīnā, sed Sextus, "Statua est salva,"
clāmat et ex hortō currit.   10

in hortum, into the garden   vexat, (he, she) annoys
sollicitus, anxious, worried   nihil, nothing
eum, him   fūrtim, stealthily
spectat, (he, she) watches   salva, undamaged, all right

13

Dress

Gaius' tunic is knee-length and, to show that he is a senator, it has a broad purple stripe running from the neck right down the front. On official occasions he wears over the tunic the **toga,** a very full garment requiring the services of two or three slaves before its folds can be successfully draped. Most Romans would wear the **toga virīlis,** a plain white toga, but Gaius has the privilege of wearing the **toga praetexta,** white with a purple edging, the distinctive dress of a senator who has held high office.

Aurelia wears a simple sleeveless white tunic and, over the tunic, a **stola**— a long, flounced dress, girdled at the waist and reaching to her ankles. For outdoor wear she adds the **palla,** a single piece of material draped around the body.

Cornelia, like her mother, is clad in the **stola.** Marcus, like his father, wears the tunic and, in public, a **toga** over it. A boy's **toga** was the same as a senior senator's—the **toga praetexta.** Both boys and girls wore around their necks a **bulla** or luck-charm which was given to them at their naming ceremony. Girls continued to wear the **bulla** until they were married. When boys came of age, at sixteen, they dedicated the **bulla** and the first scrapings of their beard to the household gods and thereafter wore the **toga virīlis.**

Romans generally went bare-headed. If protection from the wind or weather was needed, the **toga** or **palla** could be drawn over the head. Women used parasols to shield them from the sun, and men used the broad-brimmed hat (**petasus**) for this purpose.

BULLA, made of gold, bronze, lead, or leather

4
Show-off!

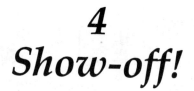

Sextus est puer molestus quī semper Cornēliam vexat. Cornēlia igitur Sextum nōn amat. Hodiē sub arbore dormit Cornēlia. Sextus puellam cōnspicit et fūrtim appropinquat. Arborem ascendit et subitō magnā vōce clāmat. Vōcem Cornēlia audit sed Sextum nōn videt. Magna vōx Cornēliam terret. Sollicita est. 5

Tum Marcus ad arborem currit. Marcus puerum molestum cōnspicit et clāmat, "Dēscende, Sexte!"

Sextus clāmat, "Marce, cūr tū nōn arborem ascendis? Nihil mē terret. Quid tē terret?"

"Cavē, Sexte!" clāmat Marcus. "Rāmī sunt īnfirmī." 10

Subitō Marcus et Cornēlia magnum fragōrem audiunt; Sextus ex arbore cadit. Rīdent Marcus et Cornēlia, sed nōn rīdet Sextus.

semper, always	**videt,** (he, she) sees
igitur, therefore	**terret,** (he, she, it) frightens
amat, (he, she) likes, loves	**tum,** at that moment, then
dormit, (he, she) sleeps	**Dēscende!** Come down!
cōnspicit, (he, she) catches sight of	**tū,** you (subject)
appropinquat, (he, she) approaches	**tē,** you (direct object)
ascendit, (he, she) climbs	**Cavē, Sexte!** Be careful, Sextus!
magnā vōce, in a loud voice	**rāmus,** (a, the) branch
vōx, (a, the) voice	**īnfirmus,** weak, shaky
audit, (he, she) hears, listens to	**fragor,** (a, the) crash, noise

In Latin, the form **Sexte** is used when Sextus is addressed by name. (Compare **Marce.**) No such change is made in English.

Exercise 4a

Respondē Latīnē:

1. Quālis puer est Sextus?   Quālis . . . ? What sort of . . . ?
2. Quid facit Cornēlia hodiē?
3. Quid facit Sextus?
4. Quid audit Cornēlia?
5. Quō Marcus currit?   Quō . . . ? Where . . . to?
6. Quid clāmat Sextus?
7. Quid audiunt Marcus et Cornēlia?

17

Exercise 4b

Select, read aloud, and translate:

1. Marcus est puer _____.
2. Sextus est puer _____.

3. Flāvia et Cornēlia in hortum _____.
4. Marcus et Sextus sunt _____.
5. Marcus nōn est _____.
6. Puerī nōn sunt _____.
7. Marcus arborem nōn _____.
8. Dāvus est vir _____.
9. Puerī _____ rīdent.
10. Cornēlia et Flāvia sunt _____.
11. _____ servī in Italiā _____.

12. Servus Britannicus _____ est quod puerī nōn _____.

Rōmānus / Rōmāna
sollicitus / sollicita/ molestus
currit / currunt
amīcus / amīcī
servus / servī
servus / servī
ascendit / ascendunt
Britannicus / Britannicī
laetus / laetī
dēfessa / dēfessae
Multī / Multae
labōrat / labōrant
īrātus / īrātī
labōrat / labōrant

NOUNS: The Ending -m

Look at these sentences taken from story 4:

Cornēlia Sextum nōn amat.
Sextus puellam cōnspicit.
Vōcem Cornēlia audit.
Marcus puerum molestum cōnspicit.

Magnum fragōrem audiunt.

Cornelia does not like Sextus.
Sextus catches sight of the girl.
Cornelia hears the voice.
Marcus catches sight of the annoying boy.
They hear a great crash.

In these sentences **Sextum, puellam, vōcem, puerum,** and **fragōrem** are the direct objects of the verbs.

The Latin nouns you have met so far end in **-m** when they are direct objects and are singular.

Versiculī: *"Serves Him Right,"* page 89.

18

Word Study I

Latin and English

Over 60% of the words in the English language come from Latin. Look again at these words from Chapter 1:

pictūra   habitat

It is not difficult to think of English words which come from them:

picture   *inhabit*

The meanings and spellings of these English words show their relationship with Latin. Such words are called *derivatives*, since they are derived from (or come from) another language, in this case, Latin.

Of course, not all of English is derived from Latin. Most of the simple words of everyday English come from Anglo-Saxon, the Germanic ancestor of English. For this reason, many modern German words sound similar to English, such as "Buch" (*book*) and "Nacht" (*night*).

English words derived from Latin are usually the longer or more difficult words. For example, consider the two English words *water* and *aquatic*. The simpler word *water* is derived from the Anglo-Saxon "waeter" and is related to the German "Wasser." The more difficult word *aquatic* comes from the Latin word for water, **aqua**. Even if one did not know the meaning of *aquatic*, Latin would help to answer the following question:

Which of these is an aquatic sport?

(a) horseback riding   (b) tennis   (c) swimming   (d) soccer

Since *aquatic* means "related to water," the correct answer is "swimming." Knowledge of Latin will help with the meanings of over 60% of the words in the English language.

Exercise 1

Below are some Latin words from Chapters 1–4. Give the meaning of each word. Then, with the meaning in mind, think of at least one English word derived from each Latin word. Use each English word correctly in a sentence.

strēnua	**sōlus**	**servus**	**agrīs**	**dēscende**
multī	**nōmine**	**spectat**	**terret**	**vōx (vōce)**

Exercise 2

Match each English word in the column at the left with its meaning in the column at the right. Use the meaning of the Latin word in parentheses as a guide.

1. chant (**cantat**)
2. sedentary (**sedet**)
3. ridicule (**rīdet**)
4. virile (**vir**)
5. elaborate (**labōrat**)
6. audible (**audit**)
7. conspicuous (**cōnspicit**)
8. dormant (**dormit**)

a. manly
b. easy to catch sight of
c. to work out carefully
d. a type of singing
e. able to be heard
f. asleep, inactive
g. to make fun of, mock
h. seated, stationary

The Dictionary

An English dictionary is a useful source not only for finding the meanings of words but also for discovering the languages from which they are derived. Not all dictionaries provide information on derivation, but most larger ones do. In these more complete dictionaries, entries may include:

a. the word
b. a pronunciation guide
c. an abbreviation indicating the part of speech
d. derivation information
e. definition(s)

Locate these items of information in the following dictionary entry:

villain (vil′ ən), n. [O.Fr. *vilain* <L.L. *vīllānus* <L. *vīlla*, a farm, country house.] 1. a baseborn or clownish person. 2. a scoundrel.

This entry shows that the English word *villain* is a noun which comes from Old French "vilain," which is from the Late Latin **vīllānus**, which derives from Latin **vīlla**, meaning a farm or country house. This derivation is especially interesting since it reveals the negative feelings toward country people that must have been prevalent at the time when the word *villain* came into use in English.

The abbreviations used in notes on derivation will be different from dictionary to dictionary. All abbreviations are explained at the beginning of each dictionary.

Exercise 3

Using a dictionary large enough to contain information on derivation, look up the following English words and copy down the complete derivation for each. Be prepared to interpret these derivations as in the example above. All of these English words are derived from Latin words you have met.

nominal   cadence   virtue   alter   ramify   infirm

5
At a Loose End

Sextus, ubi in hortum māne exit, Dāvum cōnspicit et fūrtim appropinquat. Subitō, dum Dāvus est occupātus, clāmat, "Quid tū facis, Dāve?" Dāvus, quī Sextum nōn amat, īrātus respondet, "Cūr tū mē vexās? Ego clāmōrem tuum semper audiō. Tū semper clāmās, semper rīdēs, semper curris. Ego semper sum occupātus. Ego in hortō labōrō. Ecce! Sunt multae 5 arborēs in agrīs. Sī tū puer strēnuus es, ascende arborem! Abī, moleste!" Sextus, laetus quod Dāvus est īrātus, iam in agrōs abit. Arborem magnam petit et statim ascendit. Ibi in rāmīs sedet et, "Ubi es, Marce?" clāmat. "Ecce! Ego in arbore sedeō. Ego nōn sum timidus. Nihil mē terret. Cūr tū quoque in agrōs nōn venīs? Arborēs nōn sunt magnae. Rāmī nōn sunt 10 īnfirmī."

Sed Marcus, quī adhūc dormit, Sextum nōn audit. Sextus igitur dēscendit et lentē ad vīllam redit.

ubi, when	**magnus,** big, great
māne, early in the day	**petit,** (he, she) looks for, seeks
ego, I	**statim,** immediately
clāmor, shout, shouting	**ibi,** there
tuus, your	**venīs,** you come
sum, I am	**adhūc,** still
sī, if	**redit,** (he, she) returns

Exercise 5a

Using story 5 as a guide, give the Latin for:
1. Sextus catches sight of Davus.
2. What are you doing, Davus?
3. Why do you annoy me?
4. I am working in the garden.
5. Sextus immediately climbs a big tree.
6. Marcus does not hear Sextus.

21

Exercise 5b

Read aloud and translate:

1. Sextus Dāvum saepe vexat; Dāvus Sextum nōn amat.
2. Puellae Marcum et servum cōnspiciunt.
3. Magnam vōcem Cornēlia audit.
4. Magna vōx puellam terret.
5. Sextus arborem magnam ascendit.
6. Puerī clāmōrem audiunt et statim in hortum currunt.
7. Cūr nōn sollicita es, Cornēlia? Cornēlius, pater tuus, īrātus statuam petit.
8. Dāvus, ubi clāmōrem audit, est īrātus.
9. Aestāte dum Marcus in vīllā rūsticā habitat, amīcī eius saepe ad vīllam veniunt.

eius, his

22

6
Marcus to the Rescue

Cornēlia et Flāvia in hortō saepe ambulant. Sī diēs est calidus, ex hortō in silvam ambulant quod ibi est rīvus frīgidus. In eādem silvā puerī quoque saepe errant.

Hodiē, quod diēs est calidus, puellae sub arbore prope rīvum sedent. Dum ibi sedent, Flāvia, "Cūr Marcus arborēs ascendere nōn vult? Estne puer 5 ignāvus?"

"Minimē!" respondet Cornēlia. "Cūr tū Marcum nōn amās? Marcus neque ignāvus neque temerārius est."

Tum Flāvia, "Sed Marcus est semper sollicitus. Sextum nihil terret."

Subitō lupum cōnspiciunt quī ad rīvum fūrtim dēscendit. Perterritae sunt 10 puellae. Statim clāmant, "Marce! Sexte! Ferte auxilium! Ferte auxilium!"

Puerī, ubi clāmōrem audiunt, statim ad puellās currunt. Lupus eōs iam cōnspicit et statim petit. Tum Sextus, quod lupus eum terret, arborem petit et statim ascendit. Sed Marcus rāmum arripit et lupum repellit. Puellae ē silvā currunt et ad vīllam salvae adveniunt. Brevī tempore, ubi Marcus 15 advenit, eum laetae excipiunt. Sextus, puer ignāvus, adhūc sedet in arbore perterritus. Dēscendere timet.

diēs, (a, the) day	**lupus,** (a, the) wolf
calidus, warm	**perterritus,** frightened
in silvam, into the woods	**Ferte auxilium!** Bring help! Help!
rīvus, (a, the) stream	**ad puellās,** towards the girls
frīgidus, cool	**eōs,** them
errant, (they) wander	**arripit,** (he, she) grabs hold of,
prope, near	snatches
vult, (he, she) wishes, wants	**repellit,** (he, she) drives off
ignāvus, cowardly, lazy	**ē silvā,** out of the woods
neque . . . neque . . . ,	**adveniunt,** (they) reach, arrive at
neither . . . nor . . .	**excipiunt,** (they) welcome
temerārius, rash	**timet,** (he, she) fears, is afraid

Exercise 6a

Respondē Latīnē:
1. Ubi hodiē puellae sedent?
2. Estne Marcus ignāvus?
3. Estne Marcus sollicitus?
4. Cūr puellae perterritae sunt?
5. Quid puellae clāmant?
6. Ubi clāmōrem audiunt, quid faciunt puerī?
7. Cūr Sextus arborem ascendit?
8. Quem lupus terret?   **Quem** . . . ? Whom . . . ?
9. Quid facit Marcus?
10. Quid faciunt puellae?
11. Quid facit Sextus?
12. Quālis puer est Sextus?

Exercise 6b

Select, read aloud, and translate:
1. Hodiē Sextus _____ ascendit.
   arbor / arborem
2. Sextus _____ cōnspicit.
   Marcus / Marcum
3. Nihil _____ terret.
   Sextum / Sextus
4. _____ puellae cōnspiciunt.
   Lupus / Lupum
5. Puerī _____ audiunt.
   clāmōrem / clāmor
6. _____ lupus terret.
   Sextus / Sextum
7. Sextus arborem _____ ascendit.
   magnus / magnam
8. Puellae _____ laetae excipiunt.
   Marcus / Marcum

VERBS: The Infinitive

Look at these sentences:

Arborēs **ascendere** nōn vult.   *He does not wish to climb trees.*
Dēscendere timet.   *He is afraid to come down.*

The words **ascendere** and **dēscendere** are present infinitives. The present infinitive is a form of the verb that can be recognized by the ending *-re* and may be translated by "to . . . ," e.g., **errāre**, "to wander."

Exercise 6c

Read aloud and translate:
1. Ego ad hortum currō quod Dāvum vexāre volō.
2. Puellae saepe cantant, sed Sextus cantāre nōn potest.
3. Ego arborem nōn ascendō quod in rīvum cadere nōlō.
4. Quod diēs est calidus, tū prope rīvum errāre parās.
5. Lupus ad vīllam fūrtim appropinquat; servus eum repellere nōn potest.
6. Sextus ex arbore dēscendere nōn vult quod lupus eum terret.
7. Ego in silvā sōlus ambulāre timeō.
8. Prope piscīnam sedet puella. Advenit altera puella. Iam laetae cantant puellae.
9. Subitō statua rūstica in piscīnam cadit. Clāmant puellae.
10. Puer lupum cōnspicit, rāmum arripit, lupum repellere parat.
11. Sī diēs est calidus, Marcus ambulāre in silvam vult ubi prope rīvum frīgidum sedēre potest.
12. In hortum exīre nōlō quod in vīllā labōrāre volō.

volō, I wish, want   **potest,** (he, she) is able, can
nōlō, I do not wish   **parās,** you prepare, get ready

The Slave Market

Slaves, who were in the early days mainly prisoners of war, were plentiful, and even the poorest Roman household might own one or two. Davus had been captured in Britain and sent to Rome to be sold by auction in the Forum. When his feet were whitened with chalk by the slave-dealer, Davus was mystified, but he soon discovered that this had been done to all new arrivals from abroad. A placard was hung around his neck indicating that he was British and could read and write. He was then put on a revolving stand, and bidding for him began.

He felt pretty uncomfortable standing there like an exhibit at the cattle-market, but he put the best face on it, looking around challengingly at the bidders. Titus Cornelius, father of Gaius Cornelius, was in the Forum that day to purchase some new slaves. He did not pay much attention to the placard—mangōnēs, as slave-dealers were called, were notorious swindlers—but when he saw Davus' fine physique, fair hair, and blue eyes he made a bid of 5,000 sesterces, and Davus soon found himself beside the overseer and his new master.

By this time Titus was offering 10,000 sesterces for a Greek from Rhodes. This puzzled Davus because the fellow was a pale, half-starved individual who looked as if a hard day's work would kill him. The overseer, too, looked annoyed at this extravagant bid but said nothing. But when he heard Titus being forced up to 20,000, then 30,000, he could contain himself no longer and muttered angrily, "He's not worth half that, master!" But Titus ignored him and finally paid 35,000 for the Greek Eucleides. The odd qualifications on the placard, "skilled in geometry and rhetoric," must, Davus thought, have had something to do with the record price!

As Davus, along with the strange Greek, was packed on a cart with some tough-looking Thracians also bought that day, he was filled with fear and doubt as to what might happen to him. But he needn't have worried. Old Titus proved to be the kindest of masters, and now, thirty years later, Davus, himself a grizzled fifty-five, was overseer to Gaius. On some of the neighboring farms, he knew, things were not so good.

26

7
Bad News

In vīllā sedet vir Rōmānus, nōmine Gāius Cornēlius, quī est pater Marcī et Cornēliae. Cornēlius est senātor Rōmānus. Sōlus sedet quod multās epistulās scrībere vult. Dum pater occupātus est, Marcus et Sextus et Cornēlia in agrīs vīcīnīs errant. Ibi multōs servōs labōrantēs spectant. Subitō nūntium cōnspiciunt quī ad eōs venit. Nūntius, ubi advenit, 5 puerōs salūtat.

"Salvē!" respondet Marcus. "Quem tū petis?"

Nūntius, "Gāium Cornēlium petō," inquit.

Marcus, "Gāius Cornēlius est pater meus," inquit. "Est in vīllā." Nūntium in vīllam dūcit et patrem petit. 10

"Pater," inquit Marcus, "nūntius in vīllā est."

Cornēlius statim venit et nūntium salūtat. Epistulam nūntius trādit. Cornēlius, ubi epistulam legit, "Ēheu!" inquit. "Prīnceps senātōrēs Rōmānōs ad urbem revocat. Eōs cōnsulere vult. Necesse est ad urbem redīre."

"Eugepae!" clāmat Sextus, quī Rōmam redīre vult. Gemit Cornēlia quod 15 Flāvia ad urbem venīre nōn potest.

scrībere, to write	**trādit**, (he, she) hands over
labōrantēs, working	**legit**, (he, she) reads
nūntius, messenger	**Ēheu!** Alas!
salūtat, (he, she) greets	**prīnceps**, the emperor
Salvē! Greetings! Good morning! Hello!	**ad urbem**, to the city
	revocat, (he, she) recalls
inquit, (he, she) says	**cōnsulere**, to consult
meus, my	**necesse est**, it is necessary
dūcit, (he, she) leads, takes	**Eugepae!** Hurray!

Exercise 7a

Respondē Latīnē:
1. Ubi sedet Cornēlius?
2. Cūr Cornēlius sōlus sedet?
3. Ubi Marcus et Sextus et Cornēlia errant?
4. Quōs spectant in agrīs? **Quōs** . . . ? Whom . . . ? (plural)
5. Quis advenit?
6. Quem nūntius petit?
7. Quō Marcus nūntium dūcit?
8. Cūr prīnceps senātōrēs Rōmānōs ad urbem revocat?
9. Quis clāmat "eugepae"? Cūr?
10. Cūr gemit Cornēlia?

NOUNS: The Endings -ās, -ōs, -ēs

Look at these three sentences:

Multās epistulās scrībit.	*He writes many letters.*
Multōs servōs spectant.	*They watch many slaves.*
Senātōrēs Rōmānōs revocat.	*He recalls the Roman senators.*

The words **epistulās, servōs,** and **senātōrēs** introduce you to new endings. You already know that most singular Latin nouns end in **-m** when they are used as direct objects. Plural nouns used as direct objects usually end in **-s,** e.g., **epistulās, servōs,** and **senātōrēs.**

Exercise 7b

Using story 7 as a guide, give the Latin for:
1. Cornelius is the father of Marcus and Cornelia.
2. Cornelius wants to write many letters.
3. Marcus and Sextus watch many slaves working in the fields.
4. The messenger greets the boys.
5. The messenger is looking for Gaius Cornelius.
6. Marcus looks for (his) father.
7. The messenger hands over a letter.
8. It is necessary to return to the city immediately.
9. Sextus wishes to return to Rome, but Flavia cannot.

NOUNS: Cases and Declensions

Nominative and Accusative Cases

The form of the Latin noun when used as the *subject* of a verb is known as the *nominative case*.

The form of the Latin noun when used as the *direct object* of a verb is known as the *accusative case*.

For example:

Nominative

Lup*us* eum terret.
The wolf frightens him.
Lup*ī* puerōs terrent.
The wolves frighten the boys.

Accusative

Puellae lup*um* vident.
The girls see the wolf.
Servī lup*ōs* repellunt.
The slaves drive back the wolves.

The nouns you have met so far belong to three groups or declensions:

Number Case	*1st* *Declension*	*2nd* *Declension*		*3rd* *Declension*	
Singular					
Nominative	puell*a*	serv*us*	puer	pater	vōx
Accusative	puell*am*	serv*um*	puer*um*	patr*em*	vōc*em*
Plural					
Nominative	puell*ae*	serv*ī*	puer*ī*	patr*ēs*	vōc*ēs*
Accusative	puell*ās*	serv*ōs*	puer*ōs*	patr*ēs*	vōc*ēs*

Be sure to learn these forms thoroughly.

Notes

1. In the 2nd declension, most nouns end in *-us* in the nominative singular (e.g., **servus**), but there are a few like **puer**, **ager**, and **vir** which end in *-r*. In both types, however, the accusative singular ends in *-um* and the accusative plural in *-ōs*.

2. Although **arbor**, **pater**, and **māter** end in *-r*, their other endings put them in the 3rd declension.

3. In the 3rd declension, you will note that the nouns you have met can end in different ways in the nominative singular (e.g., **arbor**, **prīnceps**, **urbs**, **pater**, **vōx**). Nevertheless, their accusative singulars all end in *-em*, and both nominative and accusative plurals end in *-ēs*.

30

Building Up the Meaning I

When you are reading a Latin sentence, each word *as you meet it* gives you certain clues about its own meaning and about what is likely to come next. First you recognize the basic meaning of the word, and then you note the case of the word, since the case will help you decide what the function of the word is in the sentence.

Consider the following sentences:

1. **Servus currit.**
The first word we meet is **servus.** We know that it is the subject of the verb because we recognize that it is in the nominative case. We can expect a verb which will tell us what the slave is "doing."

2. **Servus Dāvum cōnspicit.**
We go from **servus** to **Dāvum** and recognize **Dāvum** as accusative case. It is likely that the slave is "doing" something to Davus and that a verb will follow to tell us what the slave is "doing" to Davus.

3. **Dāvum puerī vexant.**
The first word we meet is **Dāvum.** We know that it is the direct object of the verb because we recognize it as accusative case. It is likely that someone is doing something to Davus. The next word is **puerī.** We recognize that it is nominative, and therefore it is *the boys* who are doing something to Davus. The verb **vexant** tells us what they are doing.

4. **Rāmum arripit.**
We know immediately that someone is doing something to a branch, but, since there is no noun in the nominative case, the *ending* of the verb indicates the subject and the *meaning* of the verb completes the sense.

Exercise 7c

Read aloud and translate:
1. Lupus puellās terret.
2. Puellae silvam amant.
3. Aestāte arborēs Sextus ascendere vult.
4. Dāvum et servōs puerī vexāre timent.
5. Lupī puerōs et puellās semper terrent.
6. Clāmōrēs puerī audiunt; puellās petunt.
7. Servī lupōs ex agrīs repellunt.
8. Senātōrēs Rōmānī nūntiōs salūtant.
9. Senātōrēs Rōmānōs prīnceps cōnsulere vult.
10. Cornēlius, ubi nōn est occupātus, per agrōs errāre potest.

31

Building Up the Meaning II

In 3rd declension nouns the ending of both the nominative and accusative plural is *-ēs*. To decide which case is being used, you must look for further clues. Study these sentences, and, with the help of the clues, translate them:

1. Puerī clāmōrēs audiunt.
2. Puerōs clāmōrēs terrent.

3. Prīnceps senātōrēs ad urbem revocat.
4. Prīncipem senātōrēs excipiunt.

5. Clāmōrēs mātrēs audiunt.

In sentence 1, since **puerī** is in the nominative case and is therefore the subject of the verb, **clāmōrēs** must be in the accusative case and is therefore the direct object.

In sentence 2, since **puerōs** is accusative, **clāmōrēs** must be nominative.

In sentence 3, since **prīnceps** is nominative, **senātōrēs** must be accusative. An additional clue is the fact that the verb **revocat** is singular.

In sentence 4, since **prīncipem** is accusative, **senātōrēs** must be nominative. An additional clue is the fact that the verb **excipiunt** is plural.

In sentence 5, where both nouns end in *-ēs* and the verb is plural, it is the sense which indicates that **clāmōrēs** is accusative and **mātrēs** nominative.

Exercise 7d

Explain the clues in these sentences, read aloud, and translate:
1. Servus senātōrēs videt.
2. Arborēs puerī saepe ascendunt.
3. Clāmōrēs puellās terrent.
4. Patrem vōcēs vexant.
5. Vōcēs in hortō audit.
6. Mātrēs in viā cōnspiciunt.

Versiculī: *"Show-Off!"* page 89.

Review I

Exercise Ia

Change nominatives to accusatives and accusatives to nominatives, keeping the same number (singular or plural):

1. nūntius	5. lupus	9. puerōs
2. amīcam	6. virum	10. patrem
3. fragōrem	7. rīvī	11. rāmī
4. puellae	8. vōcem	12. clāmōrēs

Exercise Ib

Change singular subjects to plural and plural subjects to singular, and make the necessary changes in the endings of the verbs:

1. Servus clāmat.
2. Puellae cantant.
3. Virī sedent.
4. Puer ad vīllam advenit.
5. Lupus rīvum petit.

6. Nūntiī in agrīs currunt.
7. Vōx puerum terret.
8. Puella amīca est.
9. Servī fragōrem audiunt.
10. Nūntius puerum cōnspicit.

Exercise Ic

Select the appropriate adjective from the pool below to complete each of the following sentences. Be sure to use the right ending on the adjective. Translate each sentence.

1. Dāvus _____ est, quod puerī clāmant.
2. Sextus arborem ascendit, quod _____ est.
3. Flāvia in vīllā _____ habitat.
4. Marcus _____ rāmum arripit et lupum repellit.
5. Dāvus puerōs _____ in piscīnā cōnspicit.
6. Dāvus _____ est, quod Sextus in hortō ambulat.
7. Flāvia et Cornēlia puellae _____ sunt et saepe in agrīs currunt.
8. Sextus est puer _____ et puellās terret.
9. Ubi lupus venit, Sextus in arbore sedet, quod puer _____ est.
10. Cornēlius _____ sedet, quod epistulās scrībere vult.

sollicitus	madidus	temerārius	vīcīnus
strēnuus	ignāvus	sōlus	
īrātus	molestus	magnus	

33

Exercise Id

Read the following passage and answer the questions below in Latin:

Hodiē quod pater Marcum ad vīcīnam urbem dūcit, Sextus in agrōs
sōlus errat. Ibi arborēs ascendere potest. Ibi servōs in agrīs labōrantēs
spectāre potest. Subitō, dum per agrōs ambulat, clāmōrēs magnōs
audit quī eum terrent. Currit ad arborem quae prope rīvum est. Celeriter ascendere parat sed, quod perterritus est et rāmī sunt īnfirmī, 5
statim in rīvum cadit.

"Ferte auxilium!" clāmat. "Celeriter venīte! Ego natāre nōn possum."

Servī, ubi clāmōrēs audiunt, statim ad rīvum currunt, rāmōs ar-
ripiunt, ad Sextum extendunt. Sextus rāmum arripit. Tum servus quī 10
rāmum tenet ad rīpam Sextum trahere potest. Sextus madidus ex rīvō
exit lacrimāns. Servī miserum puerum spectant et rīdent.

"Cūr in rīvō natās?" inquiunt.

Sextus, quī servōs saepe vexat, respondēre nōn potest et miser ad
vīllam abit. Dum per agrōs currit, servōs rīdentēs audit. 15

in agrōs, into the fields	**tenet**, (he, she) holds
per agrōs, through the fields	**rīpa**, river bank
quī, which	**trahere**, to drag, pull
celeriter, quickly	**lacrimāns**, weeping
natāre, to swim	**miser**, wretched
extendunt, (they) stretch out	**rīdentēs**, laughing

 1. Why is Sextus roaming in the fields by himself?
 2. What two things is he able to do in the fields?
 3. What frightens him?
 4. What action does he take?
 5. Why doesn't he succeed in climbing the tree?
 6. Why is he upset when he falls into the stream?
 7. How do the slaves help him?
 8. What is Sextus doing as he gets out of the stream?
 9. What do the slaves ask him?
10. Why doesn't Sextus reply?
11. How do the slaves show their feelings about Sextus?

Exercise Ie

*Locate the following in sequence as they occur in the Latin passage in
Exercise Id:*

1. All singular verbs; all plural verbs.
2. All nouns in the nominative singular, the accusative singular, the nominative plural, and the accusative plural.
3. All infinitives.

The Roman Villa

In cities, the majority of Romans lived in apartment buildings called īnsulae, which were several stories high; Cornelius, on the other hand, being a wealthy Roman, owned a self-contained house called a **domus**. We shall learn more of these town houses when Cornelius and his family reach Rome.

Like other rich Romans, Cornelius also had a house in the country. His farmhouse or **vīlla rūstica** near Baiae in Campania was similar to one actually discovered at Boscoreale near Pompeii. The ground plan of that **vīlla** is shown on the next page. The lower illustration on the next page includes the **piscīna** in Cornelius' **vīlla**.

The **vīlla** itself served two purposes: it housed the slaves who did the agricultural work, and it provided accommodation for the owner and his family when they went to the country from Rome, which they would usually do during the summer months to escape the noisy bustle and heat of the city. In addition to housing the owner's family and slaves, the **vīlla rūstica** had stables, two enclosed courts or farmyards, rooms for pressing grapes and olives, and an adjacent area for threshing.

Various features of the **vīlla rūstica** are described as follows by an ancient author who wrote a book on farming:

> The room of the overseer (**vīlicus**) should be near the entrance, and he should know who enters or leaves at night and what he is carrying, especially if there is no doorkeeper. Special care needs to be taken with the placement of the kitchen because many things are done there in the predawn hours, with food being prepared and eaten. You must see to it that the sheds in the farmyard are large enough for the wagons and all the other farming tools that might be harmed by the rain. . . . On a large farm (**fundus**) it is more convenient to have two farmyards, one with an exposed pool with running water, surrounded if you wish with columns—a sort of fishpond (**piscīna**). The cattle will drink and bathe here in the summer when brought back from plowing the fields, and also the geese, hogs, and pigs when they return from pasture. In the outer farmyard there should be a pool where lupines can be soaked along with other products that are made more fit for use by immersion in water.

Varro, *On Agriculture* I.13

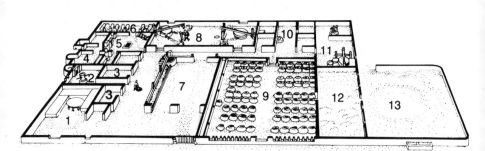

PLAN OF **VĪLLA RŪSTICA**

1. Dining Room
2. Bakery
3. Bedrooms (**cubicula**)
4. Baths
5. Kitchen
6. Stables
7. Farmyard, Court, or Garden (**hortus**)

8. Room for Pressing Grapes
9. Farmyard with Wine Vats
10. Slaves' Quarters
11. Olive-Pressing Room
12. Barn
13. Threshing Floor (**ārea**)

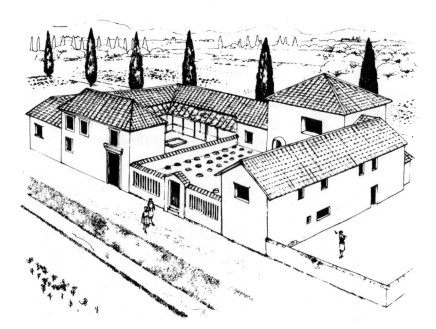

If Cornelius had been a very wealthy Roman, he might have had a country house separate from the farmhouse or even with no farm attached to it—just a large house standing in its own spacious grounds. This type of house was called a vīlla urbāna. Some Romans had more than one of these and often such houses were very luxurious indeed. The Roman author Pliny describes his Laurentine vīlla urbāna for us in a letter to a friend. Here is part of his description, and on the next page you will find a plan and a drawing of his country house:

My vīlla is large enough for my use and cheap to keep up. It has a modest entrance-hall (ātrium) through which you enter D-shaped colonnades which enclose a small but pleasant courtyard. This provides protection in bad weather, as it is sheltered by windows and overhanging eaves. In the middle of this there is a very pleasant inner court, opening into a fairly handsome dining room which juts out over the shore. On each wall there is either a folding door or an equally large window. From the sides and front there are views of the sea. Look back and there is a view of the inner court, the colonnade, the outer court, and the hall, with the woods and mountains in the distance.

Pliny, *Letters* II.17

Pliny had another vīlla urbāna in Tuscany with luxurious fountains, pools, and baths which he describes as follows:

Opposite the dining-room at the corner of the colonnade is a large bedroom. From some of its windows you look onto the terrace, from others onto the meadow, while the windows in front overlook an ornamental pool which is a pleasure both to see and hear. For the water, falling from a height, foams white in the marble basin. The bedroom is very warm in winter, being so exposed to the sun, and on a cloudy day the hot air from the nearby furnace takes the place of the sun's heat. From here you pass through a spacious and pleasant changing-room into the "cold bath" room in which there is a large bath out of the full sunlight. But if you want more space to swim in and warmer water, there is a pool in the courtyard and near it a fountain in which you can cool yourself if you've had enough of the heat.

And later in the same letter he tells us why he liked this house so much:

I can relax there with fuller and more carefree enjoyment. I need never wear a toga; nobody calls from next door. All is calm and quiet, which makes the place healthy, as do the clear sky and pure air. There I enjoy health of body and mind, for I keep my mind in training by study and my body by hunting.

Pliny, *Letters* V.6

PLINY'S **VĪLLA URBĀNA**

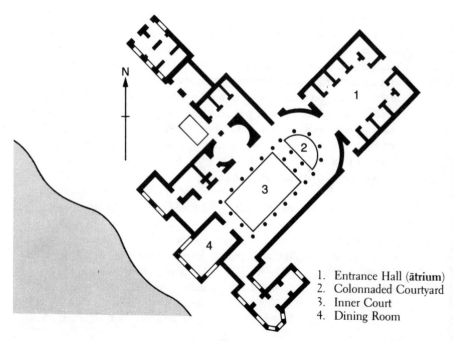

1. Entrance Hall (**ātrium**)
2. Colonnaded Courtyard
3. Inner Court
4. Dining Room

8
An Early Rise

Nōndum lūcet, sed Aurēlia, māter Marcī et Cornēliae, iam in vīllā
occupāta est. Īrāta est quod servōs sedentēs cōnspicit.
"Agite, molestī servī!" inquit. "Cūr nihil facitis? Cūr vōs ibi sedētis? Cūr
nōn strēnuē labōrātis? Omnia statim parāre necesse est quod nōs hodiē
Rōmam redīmus." Iam strēnuē labōrant servī.   5
    Tum puerōs excitāre parat. Intrat igitur cubiculum Marcī. Clāmat, "Age,
Marce! Tempus est surgere. Nōs ad urbem redīre parāmus."
    Marcus mātrem audit sed nihil respondet. Deinde Aurēlia cubiculum
Sextī intrat. Clāmat, "Age, Sexte! Tempus est surgere." Statim surgit Sextus.
Celeriter tunicam induit et brevī tempore ē cubiculō currit.   10
    Iterum Aurēlia cubiculum Marcī intrat. Iterum clāmat, "Age, Marce!
Nōs iam strēnuē labōrāmus. Cūr tū sōlus nōn surgis?"
    Gemit Marcus. "Ego nōn surgō," inquit, "quod Rōmam redīre nōlō.
Cūr mihi quoque necesse est ad urbem redīre? Patrem meum prīnceps ad
urbem revocat. Patrem cōnsulere vult. Nōn vult cōnsulere Marcum."   15
    Subitō intrat Gāius, pater Marcī, et clāmat, "Sed ego volō cōnsulere
Marcum! Cūr, Marce, hodiē mē vexās? Cūr nōn surgis? Cūr nōndum
tunicam induis, moleste puer?"
    Nihil respondet Marcus, sed statim surgit quod patrem timet.

nōndum, not yet	**intrat,** (he, she) enters
lūcet, it is light, it is day	**cubiculum,** room, bedroom
Age! Agite! Come on!	**tempus,** time
vōs, you (plural)	**surgere,** to get up
strēnuē, strenuously, hard	**deinde,** then, next
omnia, everything	**celeriter,** quickly
nōs, we, us	**induit,** (he, she) puts on
excitāre, to rouse, wake (someone) up	**iterum,** again, a second time
	mihi, for me

Exercise 8a

Respondē Latīnē:
1. Cūr est Aurēlia īrāta?
2. Cūr necesse est omnia statim parāre?
3. Quid Aurēlia in cubiculō Marcī clāmat?
4. Quid facit Marcus?
5. Surgitne Sextus?
6. Quid facit Sextus?
7. Cūr Marcus nōn surgit?
8. Quis subitō intrat?
9. Cūr Marcus surgit?

Exercise 8b

Using story 8 as a guide, give the Latin for:
1. It is necessary to work hard and prepare everything immediately because we are returning to Rome.
2. Aurelia enters Marcus' bedroom but does not wake him up.
3. "Come, Marcus! Why don't you get up?"
4. "Why do I have to return to the city?"
5. Gaius wishes to consult Marcus.

VERBS: Persons

Look at these sentences:

Rōmam redīre nōlō.	I *do not want to return to Rome.*
Cūr nōn surgi*s*?	*Why do* you *not get up?*
Aurēlia cubiculum Marcī intra*t*. Iterum clāma*t*.	Aurelia *goes into Marcus' bedroom.* She *calls again.*
Ad urbem redīre parā*mus*.	We *are preparing to return to the city.*
Cūr nōn strēnuē labōrā*tis*?	*Why do* you *not work hard?*
Līberī in agrīs erra*nt*. Servōs labōrantēs specta*nt*.	The children *wander in the fields.* They *watch the slaves working.*

The ending of the verb tells us who is doing something, i.e., whether the subject is 1st, 2nd, or 3rd *person*, singular or plural (I, you, he, she, it, we, you, they). In the 3rd person the subject may be a noun (e.g., **Aurēlia** and **līberī**). The personal pronouns **ego, tū, nōs,** and **vōs** are used only for emphasis.

40

Person	Singular		Plural	
1	*-ō*	I	*-mus*	we
2	*-s*	you	*-tis*	you
3	*-t*	he, she, it	*-nt*	they

These personal endings always have the same meaning wherever they occur.

Person	Singular		Plural	
1	par*ō*	I prepare	parā*mus*	we prepare
2	parā*s*	you prepare	parā*tis*	you prepare
3	para*t*	he, she prepares	para*nt*	they prepare

Note that the vowel that precedes the personal endings is short before final *-t* and *-nt*.

The following verb is irregular, but it uses the same endings as above (except for *-m* in place of *-ō* in the first person singular).

Person	Singular		Plural	
1	su*m*	I am	su*mus*	we are
2	e*s*	you are	es*tis*	you are
3	es*t*	he, she, it is	su*nt*	they are

Be sure to learn all of the forms above thoroughly.

Exercise 8c

Take parts, read aloud, and translate:

1. NĀRRĀTOR: Sextus est laetus.
   MARCUS: Tū es laetus, Sexte. Cūr?
   SEXTUS: Ego sum laetus quod Rōmam redīre volō.
2. NĀRRĀTOR: Servī sunt dēfessī.
   MARCUS: Vōs estis dēfessī, servī. Cūr?
   SERVĪ: Dēfessī sumus quod strēnuē labōrāmus.
3. NĀRRĀTOR: Cornēlius epistulās legit.
   CORNĒLIA: Quid legis, Cornēlī?
   CORNĒLIUS: Epistulās legō.

41

4. NĀRRĀTOR: Marcus rāmum arripit.
    SEXTUS: Quid arripis, Marce?
    MARCUS: Rāmum arripiō.
5. NĀRRĀTOR: Cornēlia rīdet.
    FLĀVIA: Cūr rīdēs, Cornēlia?
    CORNĒLIA: Rīdeō quod laeta sum.
6. NĀRRĀTOR: Senātōrēs ad urbem redeunt.
    AURĒLIA: Cūr ad urbem redītis, senātōrēs?
    SENĀTŌRĒS: Redīmus quod prīnceps nōs cōnsulere vult.
7. NĀRRĀTOR: Puerī lupum nōn timent.
    PUELLAE: Cūr lupum nōn timētis, puerī?
    PUERĪ: Lupum nōn timēmus quod temerāriī sumus.
8. NĀRRĀTOR: Puellae cantant.
    PUERĪ: Cūr cantātis, puellae?
    PUELLAE: Cantāmus quod laetae sumus.

Exercise 8d

Read aloud and translate:
1. Cūr ē vīllā in silvam saepe ambulātis, puellae?
2. In eādem silvā puerī quoque ambulant.
3. Īrāta sum quod servōs sedentēs cōnspiciō.
4. Cūr sedēs adhūc in arbore, Sexte?
5. Arborēs ascendimus quod lupī nōs terrent.
6. "Sexte! Marce!" clāmat Cornēlia. "Cūr nōn surgitis?"
7. "Ēheu!" inquit Dāvus. "Semper ego labōrō; semper mē vexant puerī; ad Britanniam redīre volō."
8. Omnia parāmus quod Rōmam hodiē redīmus.
9. Puerōs excitō quod ad urbem redīre hodiē parāmus.
10. Servī in vīllā sedent; neque Aurēliam audiunt neque respondent, nam dēfessī sunt.

nam, for

Versiculī: *"Time to Go Home,"* page 90.

Word Study II

Latin Verbs into English Verbs

Often Latin verbs come into English with only minor changes. Some verbs drop the letters *-āre, -ēre, -ere,* or *-īre* from the infinitive and replace them with silent *-e*. For example, **excitāre** (to rouse) becomes *excite* in English. Other verbs simply drop these letters from the infinitive. For example, **dēscendere** (to go down) produces the English *descend*.

Sometimes additional minor spelling changes occur. For example, **exclāmāre** (to shout out) becomes *exclaim* in English, adding an *i* in the process.

Exercise 1

Identify the English verbs derived from these Latin verbs. Be sure that you know the meaning of the English verb; in many cases it has the same meaning as the Latin verb.

extendere	salūtāre	revocāre	respondēre	surgere
repellere	vexāre	trādere	errāre	ascendere

Latin Verbs into English Nouns and Adjectives

A Latin verb may be the source of an English noun or adjective. For example, **errāre** (to wander) provides English with the noun *error* and the adjective *erratic*.

Exercise 2

The English words in italics below are derived from the Latin verbs in parentheses. Determine the meaning of the English word from the meaning of the Latin verb. Is the English word a noun or an adjective?

1. Cornelius was not moved by the runaway slave's *petition*. (**petere**)
2. Sextus' rude behavior was *repellent* to Cornelia and Flavia. (**repellere**)
3. With the *advent* of summer, Cornelius moves his family to their farmhouse at Baiae. (**advenīre**)
4. Cornelius was dictating a letter to his *scribe*. (**scrībere**)
5. "Sextus," scolded Eucleides, "your writing is not *legible*." (**legere**)
6. The *insurgent* senators were severely punished by the emperor. (**surgere**)
7. The Roman army found the *descent* from the mountain more difficult than the *ascent*. (**dēscendere, ascendere**)

43

One Latin Word into Many English Words

Some Latin words are the source of several English words, representing different parts of speech. For example, **urbs** (city) is the source of:

1.	*urban*	adjective, meaning "pertaining to a city"
2.	*urbane*	adjective, meaning "elegant and polished in manner" (How does this idea relate to **urbs**?)
3.	*urbanity*	noun, meaning "politeness, courtesy, the quality of being urbane"
4.	*urbanize*	verb, meaning "to change from country to city"
5.	*suburb*	noun, meaning "a residential area at the edge of a city"

Exercise 3

The words in each group below are derived from one Latin word. Identify the Latin word. With its meaning in mind, determine the meaning of each English word. Finally, give the part of speech of each English word.

1. *magnate, magnificent, magnify*
2. *contemporary, tempo, temporal*
3. *prince, principal, principally*
4. *inscribe, scribble, subscribe*
5. *paternal, paternity, patron*

Exercise 4

In the preamble to the Constitution of the United States, there are 22 different words derived from Latin, printed in italics below. Choose five of these words and look up their derivation in an English dictionary. Report on your findings to the class.

We the *people* of the *United States*, in *order* to *form* a more *perfect union*, establish *justice*, *insure domestic tranquillity*, *provide* for the *common defense*, *promote* the *general* welfare, and *secure* the blessings of *liberty* to ourselves and our *posterity*, do *ordain* and *establish* this *Constitution* for the *United States* of America.

Try this exercise on other famous passages, such as The Declaration of Independence, Lincoln's Gettysburg Address, and Martin Luther King's speech, "I Have a Dream."

9
Goodbye

Cornēlia, ubi surgit, ē vīllā suā fūrtim ambulat et per agrōs ad vīllam
amīcae currit. Nōndum lūcet, sed nihil Cornēliam terret. Nēmō eam cōnspicit. Nūllī servī in agrīs labōrant. Etiam iānitor ad iānuam vīllae dormit.
Cornēlia, quod tacitē intrat, iānitōrem nōn excitat.
Cornēlia cubiculum Flāviae tacitē intrat et eam excitāre temptat. Adhūc   5
dormit Flāvia. Iterum temptat Cornēlia. Flāvia sēmisomna, "Quis es? Cūr
mē vexās?"
    Cornēlia respondet, "Sum Cornēlia! Surge!"
    Flāvia surgit. Laeta Cornēliam excipit et clāmat, "Quid tū hīc?"
    Cornēlia, "Tacē, Flāvia! Nōlī servōs excitāre! Venī tacitē mēcum in agrōs.   10
Ibi nēmō nōs audīre potest."
    Cornēlia Flāviam fūrtim ē vīllā in agrōs dūcit. Ubi puellae ad arborēs
adveniunt, Cornēlia, "Misera sum," inquit, "quod ego et Marcus et Sextus
et pater et māter Rōmam hodiē redīre parāmus. Prīnceps patrem meum
cōnsulere vult. Nōbīs igitur necesse est statim discēdere."   15
    Flāvia clāmat, "Cūr statim, Cornēlia? Cūr nōn pater tuus discēdit sōlus?
Cūr vōs omnēs simul discēditis?"
    Respondet Cornēlia, "Nesciō, Flāvia. Sed nōbīs secundā hōrā discēdere
necesse est."
    Flāvia lacrimat, "Ō mē miseram! Vōs omnēs Rōmam redītis. Mihi ne-   20
cesse est hīc manēre. Valē, Cornēlia! Multās epistulās ad mē mitte! Prō-
mittisne?"
    Cornēlia, "Ego prōmittō. Et iam valē!" Cornēlia Flāviam complexū tenet
et lacrimāns abit.

suā, her own	**discēdere,** to go away
per agrōs, through the fields	**vōs omnēs,** all of you
nēmō, no one	**simul,** together
nūllī, no	**nesciō,** I do not know
iānitor, doorkeeper	**secundā hōrā,** at the second hour (of
ad iānuam, at the door	daylight)
tacitē, silently	**lacrimāre,** to weep, cry
temptāre, to try	**Ō mē miseram!** Poor me! Oh dear
sēmisomna, half-asleep	me!
hīc, here	**manēre,** to remain
Tacē! Be quiet!	**Valē!** Goodbye!
Nōlī . . . excitāre! Don't wake	**mittere,** to send
(someone) up!	**prōmittere,** to promise
mēcum, with me	**complexū,** in an embrace
misera, unhappy, miserable	**tenet,** (he, she) holds
nōbīs, for us	**lacrimāns,** weeping

Exercise 9a

Respondē Latīnē:
1. Quō Cornēlia currit?
2. Cūr nēmō Cornēliam cōnspicit?
3. Quid facit iānitor?
4. Quid facit Cornēlia ubi cubiculum Flāviae intrat?
5. Quō Cornēlia Flāviam dūcit?
6. Quis lacrimāns abit?

Prepositions

Look at the examples in the columns below:

In vīll**am** currit.
He runs into the house.

In vīll**ā** sedet.
He sits in the house.

In rīv**um** cadit.
He falls into the river.

In rīv**ō** natat.
He swims in the river.

In rām**ō** sedet.
He sits on the branch.

In urb**em** venit.
He comes into the city.

Prīnceps in urb**e** est.
The emperor is in the city.

In the left-hand column, **in** is used with the *accusative case* and the meaning is "into."

In the right-hand column, **in** is used with the *ablative case* and the meaning is "in" or "on."

Other prepositions that you have seen with the accusative case are **ad**, **per**, and **prope**.

Ad vīllam redit.
He returns to the house.

Ad iānuam dormit.
He sleeps at the door.

Per agrōs currit.
He runs through the fields.

Puellae prope rīvum sedent.
The girls sit near the stream.

Other prepositions that you have seen with the ablative case are **sub** and **ex**:

Sub arbore dormit.
He sleeps under the tree.

Ex arbore cadit.
He falls out of the tree.

Note that **ex** may be written simply as **ē** when the next word begins with a consonant: **ē rāmīs,** "out of the branches."

From now on, Latin prepositions in the word lists will indicate in parentheses whether they are followed by the accusative or the ablative case, e.g., **ad** (+ *acc.*) and **sub** (+ *abl.*).

NOUNS: Cases and Declensions

Ablative Case

Here is a table showing the groups of nouns and cases you have met so far:

Number Case	*1st* *Declension*	*2nd* *Declension*		*3rd* *Declension*	
Singular					
Nominative	puell*a*	serv*us*	puer	pater	vōx
Accusative	puell*am*	serv*um*	puer*um*	patr*em*	vōc*em*
Ablative	puell*ā*	serv*ō*	puer*ō*	patr*e*	vōc*e*
Plural					
Nominative	puell*ae*	serv*ī*	puer*ī*	patr*ēs*	vōc*ēs*
Accusative	puell*ās*	serv*ōs*	puer*ōs*	patr*ēs*	vōc*ēs*
Ablative	puell*īs*	serv*īs*	puer*īs*	patr*ibus*	vōc*ibus*

Be sure to learn these forms thoroughly.

Note that the only difference between the nominative and ablative singular endings of 1st declension nouns is that the ablative has a long vowel: *-ā.*

47

Exercise 9b

Select, read aloud, and translate:

1. Marcus ad _____ sedet.　　arborem / arbore
2. Puellae ē _____ ad _____ ambulant.　　silvam / silvā　villam / villā
3. Multī servī in _____ labōrant.　　agrōs / agrīs
4. Cornēlia amīcam ē _____ in _____ dūcit.　　villam / villā　agrōs / agrīs
5. Servus sub _____ dormit.　　statuam / statuā
6. Puerī per _____ natant.　　rīvum / rīvō
7. Cornēlius ad _____ redīre parat.　　urbem / urbe
8. Flāvia prope _____ sedet.　　arbore / arborem
9. Sextus madidus ē _____ exit.　　rīvō / rīvum
10. Geta per _____ festīnat.　　agrīs / agrōs

natāre, to swim　　festīnāre, to hurry

Exercise 9c

Read aloud and translate:

1. Marcus in villam currit. Nūntius in villā est.
2. Dāvus in hortō labōrat. Marcus in hortum festīnat.
3. Nūntius in Italiam redīre vult. Cornēlius in Italiā habitat.
4. Puer in arbore sedet. Puella in villam intrat.
5. In agrīs puerī ambulāre parant. Puellae in agrōs lentē ambulant.
6. In Italiā sunt multī servī. Aliī in agrīs labōrant, aliī in urbibus.
7. Servī sub arboribus sedēre volunt.
8. Servus ex arbore cadit; ad villam currit; in villā dormit.
9. Aliī nūntiī ex urbe celeriter veniunt; aliī ad urbem redeunt.
10. Puellae sub rāmīs sedent. Lupus ad puellās currit.
11. Puer ex arbore dēscendere nōn potest.
12. Cornēlia per iānuam in villam Flāviānam fūrtim intrat.

aliī . . . aliī . . . , some . . . others . . .

Exercise 9d

Select, read aloud, and translate:

1. Flāvia clāmat, "Ubi _____, estis / es
   Cornēlia?"
2. Cornēlia iānitōrem nōn   excitāre / excitat / excitās
   _____.

3. Nōs omnēs hodiē Rōmam   redīre / redīmus / redītis
   _____.

4. Cūr vōs omnēs simul   discēdere / discēdimus / discēdere
   _____?   parātis
5. Cūr patrem _____, Marce?   vexō / timēs / amātis
6. Necesse est epistulās statim   trādit / legere / legimus
   _____.

7. Prīnceps senātōrēs _____.   cōnsulere vult / cōnsulere volunt
8. Tacē, Flāvia! Nōlī servōs   excitāmus / excitāre / surgere
   _____.

9. Cornēlia amīcam in agrōs   adveniunt / dūcit / amat
   _____.

10. Cūr per agrōs _____,   curritis / excitātis / curris
    puellae?
11. Iānitor Cornēliam nōn   audiō / audiunt / audit
    _____.

12. Ego nōn _____ quod   dormīmus / surgere / surgō
    Rōmam redīre _____.   nōlō / faciunt / vidētis
13. _____ Cornēlia in agrīs nōn Servōs / Servī / Servus
    cōnspicit.
14. Nōlī _____ excitāre!   puellās / puellae / puella
15. Senātōrēs _____ omnēs in   Rōmānōs / Rōmānī / Rōmānum
    urbe sunt.

Exercise 9e

Using story 9 as a guide, give the Latin for:
1. Cornelia tries to wake Flavia up.
2. We are preparing to return to Rome today.
3. Why are you all leaving at the same time?
4. Send many letters to me! Do you promise?
5. Cornelia goes off in tears.

Versiculī: "Bad News," page 90.

10
Departure

Intereā in vīllā Cornēliānā omnēs strēnuē labōrant. Aurēlia multās ancillās habet. Eās iubet tunicās et stolās in cistīs pōnere. In cubiculō Marcī
servus togam praetextam in cistā pōnit quod in urbe omnēs puerī togam
praetextam gerere solent. In cubiculō Gāiī servus togam parat quod Gāius
in urbe togam gerere solet.   5

Dāvus, quī ipse omnia cūrat, ad iānuam stat. Servōs iubet cistās ē cubiculīs
in viam portāre. Baculum habet et clāmat, "Agite, servī scelestī! Dormītisne?
Hodiē, nōn crās, discēdimus."

Marcus quoque servōs incitat et iubet eōs cistās in raedā pōnere. Servus
quīdam, nōmine Geta, cistam Sextī arripit et in raedam iacit.   10

"Cavē, Geta!" exclāmat Sextus sollicitus. "Cūrā cistam meam! Nōlī eam
iacere!"

Tandem omnēs cistae in raedā sunt. Ascendunt Marcus et Sextus. Ascendit Eucleidēs. Ascendit Aurēlia. Gāius ipse ascendere est parātus. Syrus,
raedārius, quoque ascendit et equōs incitāre parat. Subitō exclāmat Aurēlia, 15
"Ubi est Cornēlia?"

Eō ipsō tempore in viam currit Cornēlia. Eam Gāius iubet in raedam
statim ascendere. Statim raedārius equōs incitat. Discēdunt Cornēliī.

intereā, meanwhile	**baculum,** a stick
ancilla, slave-woman	**scelestus,** wicked
habēre, to have, hold	**crās,** tomorrow
iubēre, to order	**incitāre,** to spur on, urge on
cista, trunk, chest	**raeda,** carriage
pōnere, to place	**servus quīdam,** a certain slave
gerere solent, (they) are accustomed	**iacere,** to throw
to wear, usually wear	**parātus,** ready
ipse, himself	**raedārius,** coachman
cūrāre, to look after, attend to	**equus,** horse
stāre, to stand	**eō ipsō tempore,** at that very
via, road	moment
portāre, to carry	

Exercise 10a

Respondē Latīnē:

1. Quid Aurēlia ancillās facere iubet?
2. Cūr togam praetextam in cistā pōnit servus?
3. Quid facit Dāvus?
4. Quid clāmat Sextus?
5. Quid raedārius facere parat?
6. Quō currit Cornēlia?
7. Quid tum facit raedārius?
8. Quid faciunt Cornēliī?

VERBS: Conjugations

Latin verbs, with very few exceptions, fall into four major groups or conjugations. You can distinguish the group or conjugation of a verb by looking at two parts—the 1st person singular of the present tense and the present infinitive. For example:

	1st Person Sing. Present Tense	Present Infinitive
1st Conjugation	par*ō*	par*āre*
2nd Conjugation	hab*eō*	hab*ēre*
3rd Conjugation	mitt*ō* iac*iō*	mitt*ere* iac*ere*
4th Conjugation	aud*iō*	aud*īre*

Note the differences between verbs of the 2nd and 3rd conjugations. Note also that some verbs of the 3rd conjugation end in *-iō* in the 1st person singular of the present tense.

Hereafter, verbs will be given in the word lists in the 1st person singular form (present tense), followed by the present infinitive and conjugation number, e.g., **habeō, habēre** (2), to have. The few exceptions that do not fit neatly into any of the four conjugations will be marked as irregular (*irreg.*).

VERBS: The Present Tense

			1st Conjugation	2nd Conjugation	3rd Conjugation		4th Conjugation
	Infinitive		par*āre*	hab*ēre*	mitt*ere*	iac*ere* (*-iō*)	aud*īre*
Number and Person	*Singular*	1	par*ō*	habe*ō*	mitt*ō*	iac*iō*	audi*ō*
		2	par*ās*	hab*ēs*	mitt*is*	iac*is*	aud*īs*
		3	par*at*	hab*et*	mitt*it*	iac*it*	aud*it*
	Plural	1	par*āmus*	hab*ēmus*	mitt*imus*	iac*imus*	aud*īmus*
		2	par*ātis*	hab*ētis*	mitt*itis*	iac*itis*	aud*ītis*
		3	par*ant*	hab*ent*	mitt*unt*	iac*iunt*	aud*iunt*

Be sure to learn these forms thoroughly.

Note that the vowel that precedes the personal endings is short before final -*t* and -*nt*.

In addition to **iaciō, iacere,** you have met the following -*iō* verbs of the 3rd conjugation:

arripiō, arripere	**excipiō, excipere**
cōnspiciō, cōnspicere	**faciō, facere**

Exercise 10b

Read the following verbs aloud and give the conjugation number and meaning of each:

ascendō, ascendere	repellō, repellere	cūrō, cūrāre
terreō, terrēre	ambulō, ambulāre	excipiō, excipere
arripiō, arripere	excitō, excitāre	timeō, timēre
discēdō, discēdere	iaciō, iacere	nesciō, nescīre
audiō, audīre	currō, currere	rīdeō, rīdēre

Exercise 10c

Using the verbs in Exercise 10b, give the Latin for the following:
1. We are running.
2. You (singular) are afraid.
3. They drive the wolf back.
4. We hear the noise.
5. You (plural) throw the chest.
6. I snatch the branch.
7. They go away.
8. They welcome the girls.
9. You (singular) frighten Cornelia.
10. We climb the tree.
11. We wake the boys up.
12. I throw the stick.
13. I run to the farmhouse.
14. They hear the voice.
15. They snatch the letter.
16. You (singular) go away.
17. You (singular) hear the noise.
18. We hear the voice.
19. We throw the stick.
20. We drive the wolf back.

VERBS: Imperative

The imperative is the part of the verb used in issuing orders, e.g.:

Cūrā cistam meam, Geta!
Take care of my trunk, Geta!

Cūrāte cistam meam, servī!
Take care of my trunk, slaves!

Nōlī eam iacere, Geta!
Don't throw it, Geta! (literally, *refuse, be unwilling to throw it, Geta!*)

Nōlīte eam iacere, servī!
Don't throw it, slaves! (literally, *refuse, be unwilling to throw it, slaves!*)

	1st Conjugation	2nd Conjugation	3rd Conjugation	4th Conjugation
Infinitive	par*āre*	hab*ēre*	mitt*ere* iac*ere* (*-iō*)	aud*īre*
Imperative Singular Plural	par*ā* par*āte*	hab*ē* hab*ēte*	mitt*e* iac*e* mitt*ite* iac*ite*	aud*ī* aud*īte*

Be sure to learn these forms thoroughly.

Exercise 10d

Read aloud and translate:
1. Dāvus omnēs strēnuē labōrāre iubet.
2. "Tunicam, nōn togam, gerere volō," clāmat Marcus.
3. In urbe Gāius togam gerere solet.
4. Eō ipsō tempore Aurēlia, "Cavē!" inquit. "Nōlī cistam iacere!"
5. Eucleidēs, "Nōlīte dormīre!" clāmat. "Strēnuē labōrāte, servī!"
6. "Cūr nōn in raedam ascenditis, puerī?" "Nōn ascendimus quod nōndum parātī sumus."
7. "Audīsne vōcem Cornēliī, Sexte?" "Ita vērō! Eius vōcem audiō."
8. Flāvia, "Scrībe ad mē saepe!" inquit. Cornēlia, "Ego prōmittō," respondet.
9. Gāius, "Ascendite, omnēs!" inquit. "Eucleidēs, cūrā puerōs! Cornēlia, sedē prope mātrem! Aurēlia, nōlī lacrimāre! Syre, incitā equōs!"
10. "Quid tū aestāte facere potes, Marce?" "Possum in agrīs currere, arborēs ascendere, in rīvō natāre, prope piscīnam sedēre."

Versiculī: *"To Rome Tomorrow," page 91.*

54

Treatment of Slaves

Some masters treated their slaves well and were rewarded by loyalty and good service, but, even when conditions were good, slaves were keenly aware of their inferior position and by way of protest sometimes rebelled or tried to run away. If they were recaptured, the letters FUG (for **fugitīvus**, "runaway") were branded on their foreheads.

Some owners treated their slaves very badly. Even if the owner were not as bad as the despised Vedius Pollio, who fed his slaves to lampreys, slaves were liable to be severely punished, often at the whim of their master:

> Does Rutilus believe that the body and soul of slaves are made the same as their masters? Not likely! Nothing pleases him more than a noisy flogging. His idea of music is the crack of the whip. To his trembling slaves he's a monster, happiest when some poor wretch is being branded with red-hot irons for stealing a pair of towels. He loves chains, dungeons, branding, and chain-gang labor camps. He's a sadist.
>
> Juvenal, *Satires* XIV.16

There were also large numbers of female slaves, and even they were often subjected to ill-treatment. Juvenal tells how a slave-woman was at the mercy of her mistress:

> If the mistress is in a bad mood, the wool-maid is in trouble, the dressers are stripped and beaten, the litter-bearers accused of coming late. The rods are broken over one poor wretch's back, another has bloody weals from the whip, and a third is flogged with the cat-o'-nine-tails. The slave-girl arranging her mistress's hair will have her own hair torn and the tunic ripped from her shoulders, because a curl is out of place.
>
> Juvenal, *Satires* VI.475

Pliny tells a story about some slaves who tried to murder their master:

> Larcius Macedo was a cruel, arrogant master, and he suffered a terrible fate at the hands of his slaves. He was taking a bath at his house at Formiae when his slaves suddenly surrounded him. One grabbed his throat while others punched him in the face, chest, and stomach. When they thought he was dead, they threw him on the hot paving-stones to see if they were right. Either because he was really unconscious or only pretending, he lay there motionless, so that they believed he was quite dead. Then he was

carried out as though he had fainted with the heat. The more loyal slaves took over; the maids came running with shrieks and screams. Roused by their cries and revived by the cool air, he opened his eyes and moved, showing that he was alive, now that it was safe to do so. The guilty slaves ran away. Most have been arrested; the rest are still being hunted. Macedo was nursed back to life, but a few days later he died. At least he had the satisfaction of knowing he was avenged. Before their victim died, the culprits suffered the penalty for murder.

Pliny, Letters III.14

On the other hand, Tacitus speaks of "slaves whose loyalty did not waver under torture." There were owners who treated their slaves fairly and sympathetically. In a letter to a friend Pliny writes:

I have noticed how kindly you treat your slaves; so I shall openly admit my own easy treatment of my own slaves. I always keep in mind the Roman phrase, "father of the household." But even supposing I were naturally cruel and unsympathetic, my heart would be touched by the illness of my freedman Zosimus. He needs and deserves my sympathy; he is honest, obliging, and well educated. He is a very successful actor with a clear delivery. He plays the lyre well and is an accomplished reader of speeches, history, and poetry. A few years ago he began to spit blood and I sent him to Egypt. He has just come back with his health restored. However, he has developed a slight cough. I think it would be best to send him to your place at Forum Julii where the air is healthy and the milk excellent for illness of this kind.

Pliny, Letters V.19

It was possible for a slave to buy his freedom if he could save enough from the small personal allowance he earned; some masters gave their slaves their freedom as a reward for long service. A slave who had been set free was called a **libertus.** Many who were freed and became rich used to hide with "patches" the marks which had been made on their bodies and faces when they were slaves.

I am very upset by illness among my slaves. Some of them have actually died, including even younger men. In cases like this I find comfort in two thoughts. I am always ready to give my slaves their freedom, so I don't think their deaths so untimely if they die free men. I also permit my slaves to make a "will," which I consider legally binding.

Pliny, Letters VIII.16

Gaius, a jurist of the second century A.D., mentions certain legal measures which were introduced to check the ill-treatment of slaves:

> But at this time neither Roman citizens nor subjects of the Empire may maltreat their slaves excessively or without good reason; for, under a regulation of the emperor Antoninus, to kill one's own slave without reason is just as serious an offense as killing another man's slave. Excessively harsh treatment by owners is also controlled by a regulation of the same emperor. He ruled that in the case of slaves who had fled for refuge to the shrines of the gods or to the statues of the emperors, the owners should be compelled to sell their slaves if their treatment was intolerably harsh.
>
> Gaius, *Institutes* 1.53

Columella, a Roman writer on agriculture, recommends securing a reliable slave as overseer (**vīlicus**) of a farm:

> I advise you not to choose an overseer from slaves who are physically attractive nor from those that have practiced the refinements of the city. These slaves are lazy and sleepy and accustomed to leisure, the Campus, the Circus, the theater, gambling, food-shops, and other such attractions and constantly day-dream of such nonsense. You should rather choose a slave hardened with farm work from infancy and tested by experience.

Friendliness and respect on the part of the master toward his slaves pay off:

> I would speak on quite familiar terms with my country slaves (if they have behaved themselves) more frequently than I would with my city slaves. And, since I have noticed that their constant toil is lightened by this friendliness of their master, I sometimes even joke with them and allow them to joke even more. Nowadays, I often consult with them about some new task as if they knew more about it than I, and this way I find out what sort of ability and intelligence each one has. Then, too, I notice that they undertake a task more willingly if they think they have been consulted about it and are undertaking it according to their own advice.
>
> Columella, *On Agriculture* I.8

11
A Slave Runs Away

Omnēs Cornēliī iam sunt in raedā. Rōmam per Viam Appiam petunt.
Intereā in vīllā Dāvus est sollicitus. Dāvus est vīlicus Cornēliī et, sī
dominus abest, vīlicus ipse vīllam dominī cūrat. Dāvus igitur omnēs servōs
in āream quae est prope vīllam venīre iubet. Brevī tempore ārea est plēna
servōrum et ancillārum quī magnum clāmōrem faciunt.   5
    Tum venit Dāvus ipse et, "Tacēte, omnēs!" magnā vōce clāmat. "Audīte
mē! Quamquam dominus abest, necesse est nōbīs strēnuē labōrāre."
    Tum servī mussant, "Dāvus dominus esse vult. Ecce! Baculum habet.
Nōs verberāre potest. Necesse est igitur facere id quod iubet." Redeunt igitur
ad agrōs servī quod baculum vīlicī timent.   10
    Sed nōn redit Geta. Neque vīlicum amat neque īram vīlicī timet. Illā
nocte igitur, quod in agrīs nōn iam labōrāre vult, cibum parat et ē vīllā
effugit. Nēmō eum videt, nēmō eum impedit. Nunc per agrōs, nunc per
viam festīnat. Ubi diēs est, in rāmīs arboris sē cēlat. Ibi dormit.
    Intereā, quamquam nōndum lūcet, Dāvus omnēs servōs excitat. In agrōs   15
exīre et ibi labōrāre eōs iubet. Sed Getam nōn videt. Ubi est Geta? Dāvus
igitur est īrātus, deinde sollicitus. Ad portam vīllae stat et viam spectat; sed
Getam nōn videt.

Via Appia, the Appian Way
vīlicus, overseer, farm manager
dominus, master
absum, abesse (*irreg.*), to be away,
    absent
ārea, open space, threshing-floor
plēnus, full
quamquam, although
mussō, mussāre (1), to mutter
verberō, verberāre (1), to beat

id quod, that which, what
īra, anger
illā nocte, that night
cibus, food
effugiō, effugere (3), to run away,
    escape
impediō, impedīre (4), to hinder
nunc, now
sē cēlāre, to hide (himself)
porta, gate

NOUNS: Cases and Declensions
Genitive Case

Compare the following sentences:

Dāvus ad portam stat.	Dāvus ad portam **vīllae** stat.
Davus stands near the door.	*Davus stands near the door of the farmhouse.*
Servī baculum timent.	Servī baculum **vīlicī** timent.
The slaves fear the stick.	*The slaves fear the overseer's stick.*
In rāmīs sē cēlat.	In rāmīs **arboris** sē cēlat.
He hides in the branches.	*He hides in the branches of the tree.*

In the right-hand column other nouns have been added to the sentences of the left-hand column. These additional nouns are in the *genitive case*. This case is used to connect two nouns in a single phrase, e.g., **portam vīllae**. It often indicates possession, e.g., **baculum vīlicī**.

This table shows the declensions and cases you have met so far:

Number Case	*1st Declension*	*2nd Declension*		*3rd Declension*	
Singular					
Nominative	puell*a*	serv*us*	puer	pater	vōx
Genitive	puell*ae*	serv*ī*	puer*ī*	patr*is*	vōc*is*
Accusative	puell*am*	serv*um*	puer*um*	patr*em*	vōc*em*
Ablative	puell*ā*	serv*ō*	puer*ō*	patr*e*	vōc*e*
Plural					
Nominative	puell*ae*	serv*ī*	puer*ī*	patr*ēs*	vōc*ēs*
Genitive	puell*ārum*	serv*ōrum*	puer*ōrum*	patr*um*	vōc*um*
Accusative	puell*ās*	serv*ōs*	puer*ōs*	patr*ēs*	vōc*ēs*
Ablative	puell*īs*	serv*īs*	puer*īs*	patr*ibus*	vōc*ibus*

Be sure to learn these forms thoroughly.

Hereafter, nouns will be given in the word lists as follows: **puella, -ae** (*f*); **servus, -ī** (*m*); **vōx, vōcis** (*f*); i.e., the nominative singular (**puella**), the genitive singular (**puellae**), and the gender (*feminine*).

N.B. It is the genitive singular ending that indicates the declension to which a noun belongs.

59

Exercise 11a

Translate the following sentences, completing them where necessary with reference to the family tree:

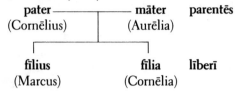

| pater | mäter | parentēs |
| (Cornēlius) | (Aurēlia) | |

| filius | filia | līberī |
| (Marcus) | (Cornēlia) | |

1. Marcus est frāter Cornēliae.
2. Cornēlia est soror Marcī.
3. Aurēlia est uxor Cornēliī.
4. Marcus est filius Aurēliae.
5. Cornēlia est _____ Cornēliī.
6. Cornēlius et Aurēlia sunt _____ Marcī et Cornēliae.
7. Marcus et Cornēlia sunt _____ Cornēliī et Aurēliae.
8. Aurēlia est _____ Marcī et Cornēliae.
9. Cornēlius est _____ Marcī et Cornēliae.

Exercise 11b

Supply the ending, read the sentence aloud, and translate:
1. Līberī in raedā senātor___ sunt.
2. Marcus est frāter Cornēli___.
3. Nūntius filium Cornēli___ salūtat.
4. Servī īram vīlic___ timent.
5. Effugit Geta et in rāmīs arbor___ sē cēlat.
6. Magna vōx Dāv___ eum terret.
7. Dāvus, vīlicus Cornēli___, Getam vidēre nōn potest.
8. Sī Cornēlius abest, Dāvus vīllam domin___ cūrat.
9. Magnus numerus līber___ est in āreā.

    numerus, -ī (m), number

Exercise 11c

Using story 11 as a guide, give the Latin for:
1. The overseer looks after the master's farmhouse.
2. In a short time the threshing-floor is full of slaves.
3. The slaves fear the overseer's stick.
4. Geta is afraid of Davus' anger.
5. Geta is sleeping in the branches of a tree.

Building Up the Meaning III

In the 1st and 2nd declensions, the endings of the genitive singular are the same as the endings of the nominative plural. To decide which case is used, you must look for further clues.

Look at these sentences:

1. **Celeriter redeunt servī.**

The genitive usually forms a phrase with another noun. Since **servī** is the only noun in the sentence, it must be nominative plural.

2. **Puerī pater est senātor Rōmānus.**

The word **puerī** could be genitive singular or nominative plural. It is only when we reach **pater** (which can only be nominative singular) and **est** (which is a singular verb) that we know that **puerī** must be genitive singular, forming a phrase with **pater**, i.e., "the boy's father."

3a. **In agrīs dominī servī strēnuē labōrant.**
3b. **In agrīs dominī servōs habent.**

In 3a **dominī** and **servī** cannot both be nominative plural since they are not linked by **et**. One of them, therefore, must be genitive singular. There is a second clue: the order of the words suggests that **dominī** forms a phrase with **in agrīs** and that **servī** is the subject of **labōrant**.

In 3b **dominī** could be genitive singular or nominative plural, but it makes more sense to take **dominī** as the subject of **habent** than to assume some unknown subject.

4. **In vīllā puerī sedent.**

Again, **puerī** could be genitive singular or nominative plural. Only the context will help you to decide whether the sentence means *The boys sit in the house*, or *They sit in the boy's house.*

12
Capture

Dāvus est sollicitus, nam necesse est Getam invenīre. Ubi servī effugiunt, dominī saepe vīlicōs reprehendunt. Saepe etiam eōs verberant. Cornēlius est dominus bonus, sed ubi Cornēlius īrātus est —
Servōs igitur Dāvus in āream statim convocat et rogat, "Ubi est Geta?" Nēmō respondēre potest. Dāvus igitur aliōs servōs in hortum, aliōs in agrōs, 5 aliōs in vīneās mittit. In hortō et agrīs et vīneīs Getam petunt. Neque in hortō neque in fossīs agrōrum neque in arboribus vīneārum Getam inveniunt.
Dāvus igitur servōs iubet canēs in āream dūcere. Aliī servī tunicam Getae in āream ferunt. Canēs veniunt et tunicam olfaciunt. Mox Dāvus servōs 10 cum canibus in agrōs dūcit. Lātrant canēs. Per agrōs Cornēliī, deinde per agrōs vīcīnārum vīllārum currunt. Neque rīvī neque fossae eōs impediunt. Vestīgia Getae inveniunt, sed Getam invenīre nōn possunt. Tandem Dāvus eōs in silvam incitat.
Geta in arbore adhūc manet et ibi dormit. Canēs lātrantēs eum excitant. 15 Nunc tamen Geta effugere nōn potest et in rāmīs sedet, immōbilis et perterritus. Canēs, ubi ad arborem appropinquant, Getam ipsum nōn cōnspiciunt, sed olfaciunt. Lātrant canēs; appropinquant servī. Miserum servum vident quī in rāmīs arboris sē cēlat.
"Dēscende, Geta!" clāmat Dāvus. Geta dēscendit. Dāvus eum tunicā 20 arripit et baculō verberat. Deinde servōs iubet Getam ad vīllam trahere et in fronte litterās FUG inūrere.

nam, for
inveniō, invenīre (4), to find
reprehendō, reprehendere (3), to blame, scold
bonus, good
convocō, convocāre (1), to call together
rogō, rogāre (1), to ask
vīnea, -ae (f), vineyard
fossa, -ae (f), ditch
canis, canis (m/f), dog
ferō, ferre (irreg.), to bring, carry

olfaciō, olfacere (3), to catch the scent of, smell
mox, soon
cum (+ abl.), with
lātrō, lātrāre (1), to bark
vestīgia, tracks, footprints, traces
tamen, however
immōbilis, motionless
tunicā, by the tunic
trahō, trahere, to drag
in fronte litterās inūrere, to brand the letters on his forehead

Exercise 12a

Respondē Latīnē:
1. Cūr est Davus sollicitus?
2. Quō Dāvus servōs mittit?
3. Inveniuntne Getam?
4. Quid canēs faciunt?
5. Cūr Geta effugere nōn potest?
6. Ubi servī litterās FUG inūrunt?

NOUNS: *Ablative Case*

The ablative case is used both with and without prepositions.

1. With a preposition, e.g.:

ē rīvō	*out of the stream*
in hortō	*in the garden*
cum patre	*with his father*
sub arboribus	*under the trees*

2. Without a preposition:

   a. Expressions referring to time, e.g.:

septimā hōrā	*at the seventh hour*
illā nocte	*on that night*
nocte	*at night*
tribus diēbus	*in three days*
aestāte	*in summer*
brevī tempore	*in a short time*

   b. Other uses of the ablative without a preposition can often be translated "by" or "with," e.g.:

Getam tunicā arripit.	*He seizes Geta by the tunic.*
Servum baculō verberat.	*He beats the slave with a stick.*

   c. Sometimes English requires a different form of expression, e.g.:

Magnā vōce clāmat.	*He shouts loudly* (literally, *in a loud voice*).
Servus, nōmine Geta, . . .	*a slave called Geta* (literally, *Geta by name*), . . .

Exercise 12b

Supply the ending, read aloud, and translate:
1. Ē vīll___ currit Gāius ipse.
2. Vīlicus ancillam tunic___ arripit.
3. Servus, nōmin___ Geta, effugit.
4. Quis togās in cist___ pōnit?
5. Per viās urbis cum patr___ ambulāre volō.
6. Dāvus servōs iubet canēs ex agr___ in āream dūcere.

Exercise 12c

Select, read aloud, and translate:

1. Geta in _____ sē cēlat.
2. Prope _____ vīllae servī stant.
3. Aliī in _____, aliī in _____ sedent.
4. Servī in fossīs _____ Getam nōn vident.
5. Dāvus servōs cum _____ in agrōs dūcit.
6. Est magnus numerus _____ et _____ in vīllā vīcīnā.
7. Ubi est vīlicus _____ _____?
8. Dāvus Getam _____ verberat.

arborem / arbore / arboris
portae / portam / porta
cubiculum / cubiculō
āreā / āreae / āream
agrīs / agrī / agrōs
canēs / canem / canibus
puerī / puerōs / puerōrum
puellārum / puella / puellam
dominus / dominō / dominī
bonō / bonī / bonum
baculum / baculī / baculō

Exercise 12d

Read aloud and translate:

1. Vōcēs servōrum in agrīs audīmus.
2. Puerōrum clāmōrēs puellae timent.
3. In vīllā senātōris Rōmānī sedent amīcae Aurēliae.
4. Sub rāmīs arboris Cornēlia sedet.
5. Omnēs Cornēliī servī vestīgia Getae petunt; brevī tempore eum inveniunt.
6. Ē cubiculō Marcī servī cistās ferunt.
7. Līberī cum patre et mātre in raedam ascendunt.
8. Magnus fragor rāmōrum puellās terret; ē rāmīs arboris cadit subitō Sextus.

Versiculī: "Spoken by Geta," page 91.

Review II

Exercise IIa

Change singulars to plurals and plurals to singulars, keeping the same case:

1. vīlicō	9. vōx	17. portārum
2. cistae (gen.)	10. fossae (nom.)	18. virōrum
3. noctem	11. cibī (gen.)	19. fragōrēs (acc.)
4. dominī (nom.)	12. patribus	20. filia
5. ancillā	13. puerum	21. raedāriīs
6. canēs (nom.)	14. raedīs	22. canis (gen.)
7. equōs	15. frontem	23. equum
8. āream	16. filius	24. arbore

Exercise IIb

Read and translate each sentence below with the appropriate form of each of the following verbs:

portō, portāre iaciō, iacere habeō, habēre
inveniō, invenīre pōnō, pōnere

1. Ego cistam _____.
2. Tū cistam _____.
3. Puer cistam _____.
4. Nōs cistam _____.
5. Vōs cistam _____.
6. Puerī cistām _____.
7. _____ cistam, puer!
8. _____ cistam, puerī!

Exercise IIc

Give the first person singular, infinitive, conjugation number, and meaning of each of the following verbs:

For example: surgimus   Answer: surgō, surgere (3), to rise

1. intrātis
2. iubēs
3. habent
4. impedīte
5. reprehendimus
6. convocā
7. rogat
8. manē
9. mussātis
10. cūrō
11. prōmittis
12. festīnāte
13. verberāmus
14. olfaciunt

Exercise IId

Read the following passage and answer the questions in Latin:

Hodiē servus novus ad vīllam Cornēliī venit. Dāvus eum ex urbe vīcīnā dūcit.

DĀVUS:	Ego sum Dāvus, vīlicus Gāiī Cornēliī. Gāius Cornēlius est senātor Rōmānus. Quod est senātor, in urbem saepe redit. Nunc Cornēlius, dominus meus, abest sed aestāte in vīllā habitat cum Aurēliā et Marcō et Cor- 5 nēliā et Sextō. Aurēlia est uxor Cornēliī.
SERVUS:	Sed quis est Marcus?
DĀVUS:	Marcus est fīlius Cornēliī et frāter Cornēliae. Cornēlia igitur est fīlia Cornēliī et soror Marcī. 10
SERVUS:	Sed quis est Sextus? Estne frāter Marcī?
DĀVUS:	Minimē vērō! Nōn est frāter sed amīcus Marcī. Pater Sextī est amīcus Cornēliī. Pater Sextī nōn in Italiā sed in Asiā habitat. Sextus cum Marcō in Italiā habitat. 15
SERVUS:	Suntne multī servī in vīllā Cornēliī?
DĀVUS:	Est magnus numerus servōrum et ancillārum. Aliī servī in vīllā labōrant, aliī in agrīs et in vīneīs et in olīvētīs.
SERVUS:	Quid faciunt ancillae? 20
DĀVUS:	Togās et tunicās līberōrum et parentum cūrant. Cibum quoque parant.
SERVUS:	Laetī sunt servī Gāiī Cornēliī. Amantne dominum?
DĀVUS:	Ita vērō! Sum vīlicus virī bonī. 25

novus, new
olīvētīs, olive groves

1. Who comes to Cornelius' farmhouse?
2. Who brings him there?
3. Why does Cornelius often return to Rome?
4. Where is Cornelius now?
5. Who is Marcus?
6. Who is Cornelia?
7. Is Sextus Marcus' brother?
8. Who is Marcus' friend?
9. Where does Sextus' father live?
10. In what four places do the slaves work?
11. What do the slave-women do?
12. What is the slaves' attitude toward their master?

67

Exercise IIe

Select the appropriate adjective from the list below to complete each of the following sentences. Be sure to use the right ending on the adjective. Translate each sentence.

1. Dāvus ad āream _____ servōrum et ancillārum advenit.
2. Gāius in raedam ascendere est _____.
3. Cornēlia Flāviam _____ excitāre temptat.
4. Servī _____ ē vīllā effugiunt.
5. Cornēlia ē vīllā _____ ambulat et ad vīllam amīcae currit.

parātus	suus	plēnus	sēmisomnus	scelestus

Exercise IIf

Complete the following sentences to match the English:

1. Cornēlia et Marcus et Sextus _____ in vīllā habitant. (in summer)
2. Marcus et Sextus _____ sedent. (under the tree)
3. Nūntius sollicitus _____ currit. (to the farmhouse)
4. Puer temerārius _____ cadit. (out of the tree)
5. Cornēlia _____ ad vīllam vīcīnam fūrtim ambulat. (that night)
6. Servus _____ dormit. (at the door)
7. Cornēlius sōlus _____ epistulam scrībit. (in the farmhouse)
8. Servī _____ per agrōs currunt. (with the dogs)
9. Puer molestus _____ cadit. (into the fishpond)
10. Dāvus _____ Getam verberat. (with a stick)

Exercise IIg

In the passage in Exercise IId above, find the Latin for:

1. the house of Cornelius
2. from the neighboring city
3. the overseer of Gaius Cornelius
4. in summer
5. the wife of Cornelius
6. the sister of Marcus
7. the friend of Marcus
8. with Marcus
9. large number of slaves and slave-women
10. in the olive groves

13
Disaster

Intereā Cornēliī per Viam Appiam iter faciēbant. Cornēlius, quod ad
urbem tribus diēbus advenīre volēbat, Syrum identidem iubēbat equōs incitāre. Syrus igitur equōs virgā verberābat. Dum per viam ībant, Aurēlia et
Cornēlia spectābant rūsticōs quī in agrīs labōrābant. Marcus et Sextus spec-
tābant omnēs raedās quae per Viam Appiam ībant.   5
Septima hōra erat. Diēs erat calidus. In agrīs rūsticī nōn iam labōrābant,
sed sub arboribus quiēscēbant. In raedā Cornēlius et Aurēlia iam dormiēbant.
Marcus pede vexābat Cornēliam quae dormīre volēbat. Sextus cum raedāriō
Syrō sedēbat; viam et vehicula spectābat.
Subitō, "Ecce, Marce!" exclāmat Sextus. "Est aurīga!"   10
Marcus magnō rīsū respondet, "Nōn est aurīga, fatue! Est tabellārius quī
epistulās cīvium praeclārōrum ab urbe fert. Tabellāriī semper celeriter iter
faciunt quod epistulās ab urbe ad omnēs partēs Italiae ferunt."
"Quam celeriter iter facit!" clāmat Sextus. "Equōs ferōciter virgā incitat.
Cavē tabellārium, Syre! Tenē equōs! Cavē fossam! Cavē fossam!"   15
Syrus equōs tenet et tabellārium vītat, sed raeda in fossam magnō fragōre
dēscendit.

iter faciēbant, (they) were traveling	**pēs, pedis** (*m*), foot
tribus diēbus, in three days	**vehicula,** vehicles
volēbat, (he, she) wanted	**aurīga, -ae** (*m*), charioteer
identidem, again and again	**magnō rīsū,** with a loud laugh
iubēbat, he ordered, kept ordering	**fatuus,** stupid
virga, -ae (*f*), stick	**tabellārius, -ī** (*m*), courier
verberābat, he kept beating, whip-	**cīvis, cīvis** (*m*), citizen
ping	**praeclārus,** distinguished
rūsticus, -ī (*m*), peasant	**ab** or **ā** (+ *abl.*), from
ībant, (they) were going	**pars, partis** (*f*), part
septimus, seventh	**Quam . . . !** How . . . !
erat, it was	**ferōciter,** fiercely
quiēscēbant, (they) were resting	**vītō, vītāre** (1), to avoid

Exercise 13a

Respondē Latīnē:
1. Quid Cornēliī faciēbant?
2. Cūr Cornēlius Syrum identidem iubēbat equōs incitāre?
3. Quid faciēbat Syrus?
4. Quid faciēbant Aurēlia et Cornēlia dum per viam ībant?
5. Cūr rūsticī nōn iam labōrābant?
6. Cūr Cornēlia nōn dormiēbat?
7. Ubi sedēbat Sextus?
8. Quis celeriter appropinquat?
9. Cūr tabellāriī celeriter iter faciunt?
10. Quō īnstrumentō tabellārius equōs incitat?
11. Vītatne Syrus tabellārium?
12. Quō dēscendit raeda?

> Quō īnstrumentō . . . ? With what instrument . . . ?
>
> How . . . ?

Exercise 13b

Using story 13 as a guide, give the Latin for:
1. Again and again Cornelius kept ordering Syrus to spur on the horses.
2. While they were going along the road, Marcus and Sextus were looking at all the carriages.
3. The day was warm and it was the seventh hour.
4. The peasants were resting under the trees, and Cornelius and Aurelia were asleep in the carriage.
5. Marcus kept annoying Cornelia again and again.
6. Sextus was looking at a courier who was going along the road.
7. Couriers quickly carry letters to all parts of Italy.
8. How fiercely he spurs on the horses with (his) stick!
9. Syrus avoids the courier but not the ditch.

70

VERBS: The Imperfect Tense

Look at these examples from the story:

Per Viam Appiam iter **faciēbant**.	*They were traveling along the Via Appia.*
Ad urbem tribus diēbus advenīre **volēbat**.	*He wanted to reach the city in three days.*
Syrus equōs **verberābat**.	*Syrus kept whipping the horses.*

The Latin verbs in dark type are examples of the *imperfect tense*. This tense is easily recognized because the letters *-ba-* appear before the personal ending.

N.B. The imperfect forms of **sum, esse** (to be) and **possum, posse** (to be able) are irregular:

erat, (he, she, it) was	**poterat,** (he, she, it) was able
erant, (they) were	**poterant,** (they) were able

Exercise 13c

Read aloud, say whether the verb is present or imperfect, and translate:
1. Cornēlia sub arbore sedet.
2. Flāvia in agrīs ambulābat.
3. Rōmānī in Italiā habitant.
4. Servī Getam invenīre nōn poterant.
5. Lātrant canēs; appropinquant servī.
6. Marcus et Sextus raedās spectābant.
7. Rūsticī erant in agrīs.
8. Puerī saepe currunt in agrīs.
9. Geta labōrāre nōlēbat.
10. Tabellāriī epistulās ab urbe in omnēs partēs Italiae ferēbant.

Versiculī: *"Disaster," page 92.*

71

Word Study III

Latin Suffix -or

The suffix -*or*, when added to the base of a Latin verb, creates a 3rd declension noun which means "the act of" or "the result of" that particular verb. The base of a verb is found by subtracting the -*āre, -ēre, -ere,* or -*īre* ending from its infinitive. For example, **clāmāre** (base: **clām-**) becomes **clāmor, clāmōris** (*m*), a shout. The Latin noun formed in this way often comes into English unchanged. The derivative *clamor* means "a loud outcry."

Exercise 1

Create a 3rd declension noun from each verb below. Give the nominative and genitive singular of the noun. Give an English derivative, if there is one.

terrēre	**tenēre**	**stupēre** (to be amazed)
errāre	**timēre**	**valēre** (to be strong)

English Suffix -(i)fy

The Latin verb **facere** (to do, make) is the source of the English verb suffix -*(i)fy*, meaning "to make." The English word *beautify* means "to make beautiful." Often the base to which the suffix is added is also of Latin origin. The Latin word **magnus** provides the base for the English word *magnify*, "to make large."

Exercise 2

Identify the English verbs made by adding the suffix -*(i)fy* to the bases of these Latin words.

terrēre	**satis** (enough)
quālis	**ūnus** (one)
nūllus	**signum** (sign)

Exercise 3

Match each English word in the column at the left with its meaning in the column at the right. Use the meaning of the Latin word in parentheses as a guide.

1. fraternity (**frāter**)
2. novelty (**novus**)
3. pedestrian (**pēs, pedis**)
4. procrastinate (**crās**)
5. ancillary (**ancilla**)
6. tacit (**tacitē**)
7. simultaneous (**simul**)
8. dominate (**dominus**)

a. unspoken
b. put off until tomorrow
c. brotherhood
d. be master over
e. traveler on foot
f. something new
g. at the same time
h. serving as helper

Latin Mottoes

Although Latin is an ancient language, its words and phrases are still part of our life today. Look at the inscriptions on a penny, nickel, dime, or quarter. Find the Latin words E PLURIBUS UNUM. This is the motto of the United States, meaning "out of many, one." It refers to the many colonies which were united to make one nation.

Many states, universities, and other organizations have Latin mottoes which serve as symbols of their purpose, for example:

SEMPER FIDELIS "always faithful" (U.S. Marine Corps)
LABOR OMNIA VINCIT "Work conquers everything." (Oklahoma)
VOX CLAMANTIS IN DESERTO "the voice of one crying in the wilderness" (Dartmouth College)
A MARI USQUE AD MARE "from sea to sea" (national motto of Canada)
GRANDESCUNT AUCTA LABORE "By work, all things increase and grow." (McGill University)

Exercise 4

Find further examples of mottoes in English, Latin, or other languages used by any of the following:

a. your home state or city
b. military units, such as the army, navy, or air force
c. local colleges, universities, or academies
d. local organizations: community service groups, political groups, unions, or clubs.

14
Who Is to Blame?

Ubi dēscendit raeda in fossam, concidunt omnēs. Nēmō tamen ē raedā cadit. Mox cūnctī in viam ē raedā dēscendunt, sollicitī sed incolumēs. Cornēlius, quamquam gaudet quod omnēs sunt incolumēs, raedārium miserum reprehendit.

"Age, Syre! Nōlī cessāre! Extrahe statim raedam ē fossā!" 5
Syrus igitur equōs incitat. Equī raedam strēnuē trahunt, sed frūstrā. Raeda in fossā haeret immōbilis. Syrus eam movēre nōn potest.

"Ō sceleste!" inquit Cornēlius. "Tuā culpā raeda est in fossā. Quid tū faciēbās ubi cisium appropinquābat? Dormiēbāsne?"

Interpellat Sextus, "Syrus nōn dormiēbat, sed per viam placidē ībat dum 10
appropinquābat cisium. Ego et Marcus spectābāmus cisium quod celerrimē appropinquābat. Deinde tabellārius equōs ad raedam nostram dēvertēbat. Perīculum erat magnum. Syrus cisium vītāre poterat et iam nōs omnēs sumus incolumēs quod Syrus raedam magnā arte agēbat."

Tum Cornēlius rogat, "Tūne cisium spectābās, Marce, ubi appropin- 15
quābat?"

"Ita vērō, pater!" respondet Marcus. "Omnia observābam. Erat culpa tabellāriī, nōn Syrī. Syrus raedam magnā arte agēbat."

Sed Cornēlius, magnā īrā commōtus, virgam arripit et raedārium miserum verberat. 20

---

concidō, concidere (3), to fall down
cūnctī, all
incolumis, unhurt, safe and sound
gaudeō, gaudēre (2), to be glad
cessō, cessāre (1), to be idle, do nothing
extrahō, extrahere (3), to drag out
frūstrā, in vain
haereō, haerēre (2), to stick
moveō, movēre (2), to move
culpa, -ae (f), fault, blame
cisium, light two-wheeled carriage

interpellō, interpellāre (1), to interrupt
placidē, gently, peacefully
quod, which
celerrimē, very fast
noster, our
dēvertēbat, he began to turn aside
perīculum, danger
ars, artis (f), skill
agō, agere (3), to drive
commōtus, moved

Exercise 14a

Respondē Latīnē:

1. Quid accidit ubi dēscendit raeda in fossam? **accidit,** happens
2. Quō cūnctī dēscendunt?
3. Cūr Cornēlius gaudet?
4. Potestne Syrus raedam ē fossā extrahere?
5. Dormiēbatne Syrus ubi cisium appropinquābat?
6. Cuius culpa erat? **Cuius . . . ?** Whose . . . ?
7. Quōmodo Syrus raedam agēbat? **Quōmodo . . . ?** In what way . . . ?
   How . . . ?
8. Quōmodo commōtus est Cornēlius?
9. Quid facit Cornēlius īrātus?

75

VERBS: The Imperfect Tense

You have now met all the endings of the imperfect tense:

	1	-bam		1	-bāmus
Singular	2	-bās	Plural	2	-bātis
	3	-bat		3	-bant

Note that the vowel is short before final -*m*, -*t*, and -*nt*.

These are the endings of the imperfect tense of *all* Latin verbs (except **esse** and its compounds, of which **posse** is one; see page 101).

The Imperfect Tense

			1st Conjugation	2nd Conjugation	3rd Conjugation		4th Conjugation
	Infinitive		par*āre*	hab*ēre*	mitt*ere*	iac*ere* (-*iō*)	aud*īre*
Number and Person	*Singular*	1	parā*bam*	habē*bam*	mittē*bam*	iaciē*bam*	audiē*bam*
		2	parā*bās*	habē*bās*	mittē*bās*	iaciē*bās*	audiē*bās*
		3	parā*bat*	habē*bat*	mittē*bat*	iaciē*bat*	audiē*bat*
	Plural	1	parā*bāmus*	habē*bāmus*	mittē*bāmus*	iaciē*bāmus*	audiē*bāmus*
		2	parā*bātis*	habē*bātis*	mittē*bātis*	iaciē*bātis*	audiē*bātis*
		3	parā*bant*	habē*bant*	mittē*bant*	iaciē*bant*	audiē*bant*

Be sure to learn these forms thoroughly.

Note that the personal endings are the same as those given for the present tense on page 41, except that in this tense the first person singular ends in -*m* (compare **sum**).

The following is a summary of the meanings of the imperfect tense:

Syrus nōn **dormiēbat**.	*Syrus* **was** *not* **sleeping**.
Cornēlia dormīre **volēbat**.	*Cornelia* **wanted** *to sleep*.
Marcus Cornēliam **vexābat**.	*Marcus* **kept annoying** *Cornelia*.
Dāvus in Britanniā **habitābat**.	*Davus* **used to live** *in Britain*.
Equōs ad raedam nostram **dēvertēbat**.	*He* **began to turn** *the horses in the direction of our coach*.

Exercise 14b

Read aloud and translate:
1. Tabellārium līberī spectābant.
2. Cornēlius, ubi epistulās scrībēbat, uxōrem et līberōs vidēre nōlēbat.
3. Gaudēbat Cornēlius quod omnēs ē raedā incolumēs dēscendēbant.
4. Prīnceps tabellāriōs ex urbe saepe mittēbat.
5. Syrus tabellārium vītāre poterat quod equōs tenēbat.
6. Dormiēbāsne, Syre? Minimē vērō, domine! Ego placidē per viam ībam.
7. Quid vōs faciēbātis, puerī? Nōs omnēs raedās spectābāmus, pater.
8. Appropinquābatne cisium placidē? Minimē! Celerrimē per viam ībat.
9. Cūr mē semper vexābās, Marce? Dormīre volēbam.

Exercise 14c

Select, read aloud, and translate:
1. Tabellārius equōs ferōciter _____.
   incitābam / incitābat / incitābant
2. Pater et māter ē raedā _____.
   dēscendēbās / dēscendēbat / dēscendēbant
3. Cūr tū celeriter iter _____?
   faciēbās / faciēbant / faciēbāmus
4. Nōs omnēs in raedā _____.
   dormiēbam / dormiēbātis / dormiēbāmus
5. Ego et Marcus saepe in agrīs _____.
   currēbāmus / currēbant / currēbat

Exercise 14d

Supply the imperfect tense endings, read aloud, and translate:
1. Tabellārius multās epistulās ab urbe portā___.
2. Cornēlia, quae dēfessa era___, in cubiculō dormiē___.
3. Nōs omnēs raedam magnā arte agē___.
4. Sub arboribus vīneārum et in olīvētīs vōs Getam petē___.
5. Latrā___ canēs; per agrōs currē___; Getam invenīre nōn
   potera___.
6. "Dāve, servumne baculō verberā___?"
7. Aliī servī in vīllā, aliī in vīneīs labōrā___.
8. Sextus identidem clāmā___, "Ecce! aurīga!"

olīvētīs, olive groves

77

15
Vehicle Spotting

Dum raeda in fossā manēbat, Marcus et Sextus vehicula exspectābant.
Longum erat silentium.
Diū nūllum vehiculum appāret. Tandem Marcus murmur rotārum audit
et procul vim pulveris cōnspicit.
Sextus, "Quid est, Marce? Estne plaustrum?"   5
Marcus, "Minimē, fatue! Plaustra onera magna ferunt. Tarda igitur sunt.
Sed illud vehiculum celeriter appropinquat."
Sextus, "Ita vērō! Praetereā equī illud vehiculum trahunt. Bovēs plaustra
trahunt. Fortasse est raeda."
"Nōn est raeda," inquit Marcus, "Nam quattuor rotās habet raeda. Illud   10
vehiculum duās tantum rotās habet."
"Est cisium!" clāmat Sextus. "Ecce, Marce! quam celeriter appropinquat!
Fortasse est alius tabellārius."
"Minimē, Sexte!" respondet Marcus. "Nōn est tabellārius. Tabellāriī
tunicās gerere solent. Ille togam gerit. Fortasse est vir praeclārus quī ab urbe 15
Neāpolim iter facit."
Praeterit cisium. Tum vim pulveris tantum vident et murmur rotārum
audiunt. Tandem silentium.

exspectō, exspectāre (1), to look out for	**tardus, -a, -um**, slow
longus, -a, -um, long	**ille, illa, illud**, that, he, she, it
diū, for a long time	**praetereā**, besides
appāreō, appārēre (2), to appear	**bōs, bovis** (m/f), ox
rota, -ae (f), wheel	**tantum**, only
procul, in the distance, far off	**fortasse**, perhaps
vim pulveris, a cloud of dust	**alius, alia, aliud**, another
plaustrum, -ī (n), wagon, cart	**Neāpolim**, to Naples
onus, oneris (n), load, burden	**praetereō, praeterīre** (irreg.), to go past

RAEDA

PLAUSTRUM

CISIUM

Numerals and Numbers

I	ūnus, -a, -um, one	VIII	octō, eight
II	duo, -ae, -o, two	IX	novem, nine
III	trēs, trēs, tria, three	X	decem, ten
IV	quattuor, four	L	quīnquāgintā, fifty
V	quīnque, five	C	centum, a hundred
VI	sex, six	D	quīngentī, -ae, -a, five hundred
VII	septem, seven	M	mīlle, a thousand

Full sets of the forms of ūnus, duo, and trēs are given on page 99.

Exercise 15a

Complete these sentences with the Latin words for the appropriate numbers, read aloud, and translate:

1. Quot rotās habet raeda? _____ rotās habet raeda.
2. Quot rotās habet cisium? _____ rotās habet cisium.
3. Quot līberī in raedā erant? _____ līberī in raedā erant.
4. Duo et _____ sunt decem.
5. Duo et trēs sunt _____.
6. Sex et _____ sunt novem.
7. Quīnque et trēs sunt _____.
8. Quattuor et sex sunt _____.
9. Quattuor et quīnque sunt _____.
10. Quattuor et _____ sunt septem.

      Quot . . . ? How many . . . ?

Neuter Nouns

Some nouns in Latin have the same ending in the accusative as in the nominative. They have **-a** as the ending in the nominative and accusative plural. These are neuter nouns.

You have met sentences like:

Davus **baculum** habet.   *Davus has a stick.*
Vestīgia Getae inveniunt.   *They find Geta's tracks.*

The words **baculum** and **vestīgia** are neuter nouns. The 2nd and 3rd declensions have neuter nouns.

Number Case	*2nd Declension*	*3rd Declension*
Singular		
Nominative	bacul**um**	nōmen
Genitive	bacul**ī**	nōmin**is**
Accusative	bacul**um**	nōmen
Ablative	bacul**ō**	nōmin**e**
Plural		
Nominative	bacul**a**	nōmin**a**
Genitive	bacul**ōrum**	nōmin**um**
Accusative	bacul**a**	nōmin**a**
Ablative	bacul**īs**	nōmin**ibus**

There are three genders of Latin nouns: masculine, feminine, and neuter. Most nouns of the 1st declension are feminine (e.g., **puella**). The 2nd declension contains both masculine nouns (such as those in the chart on page 59) and neuter nouns as in the chart on page 80. The 3rd declension contains nouns of all three genders (e.g., **pater** and **vōx** in the chart on page 59, which are masculine and feminine respectively, and **nōmen** in the chart on page 80, which is neuter).

All of this is brought together in the chart on page 97 at the end of this book, which shows the forms of nouns of all three genders in the three declensions.

Other examples of neuter nouns are:

2nd Declension	3rd Declension
auxilium, -ī (n), help	**iter, itineris** (n), journey
cisium, -ī (n), light two-wheeled carriage	**murmur, murmuris** (n), murmur, rumble
cubiculum, -ī (n), room, bedroom	**onus, oneris** (n), load
olīvētum, -ī (n), olive grove	**tempus, temporis** (n), time
perīculum, -ī (n), danger	
plaustrum, -ī (n), wagon, cart	
silentium, -ī (n), silence	
vehiculum, -ī (n), vehicle	
vestīgium, -ī (n), track, footprint, trace	

Exercise 15b

Read aloud and translate:

1. Nūllum vehiculum puerī cōnspicere poterant.
2. Nox erat; raeda in fossā immōbilis manēbat; nēmō auxilium ferēbat.
3. Marcus et Sextus spectābant vehiculum quod celerrimē appropinquābat.
4. Canis lātrābat quod murmur rotārum audiēbat.
5. Marcus baculum iaciēbat; canis baculum petēbat.
6. Plaustra onera magna ferēbant.
7. Erant multa vehicula in viā; cisium tarda vehicula praeterībat.
8. "Quot vehicula vidēre potes, Marce?" rogat Sextus. "Ūnum cisium et tria plaustra procul videō."
9. Vestīgia vehiculōrum vidēre poterāmus, nam via erat madida.
10. Quot līberōs in raedā vidēs? In raedā ūnam puellam et duōs puerōs videō.
11. Quot līberī Rōmam raedā iter faciēbant? Ūna puella et duo puerī cum parentibus Rōmam ībant.
12. Raedārius baculō equōs incitat; equī celerrimē currunt.
13. Nescīmus nōmina omnium servōrum; sed Dāvus cūnctōs servōs nōmine saepe convocābat.
14. Quamquam tabellāriī multa itinera faciēbant, perīcula magna in viīs identidem vītābant.

Word Study IV

Numbers

The Latin words for numbers provide English with a great many words. For example, the English word *unite* (to bring together as *one*) comes from the Latin number **ūnus**. The English word *duet* (music for *two* performers) is derived from **duo** in Latin, and *triple* (*three* fold) traces its ancestry to the Latin **trēs**.

Exercise 1

Match these English words with their meanings.

1.	sextet	a.	five babies born together
2.	unique	b.	an eight-sided figure
3.	decimate	c.	one-of-a-kind, without equal
4.	quadrant	d.	people in their seventies
5.	duplex	e.	to destroy one tenth of
6.	septuagenarians	f.	a set of three
7.	octagon	g.	one fourth of a circle
8.	triad	h.	a period of 100 years
9.	quintuplets	i.	a group of six
10.	century	j.	a two-family house or an apartment on two levels

The Roman Number System

The origin of Roman numerals from one to ten is in the human hand. The Roman numeral **I** is one finger held up; the numeral **II** is two fingers, and so on. The numeral **V** comes from the v-shape between the thumb and the other four fingers pressed together, and it therefore represents five. When two V's are placed with their points touching, the numeral **X** is formed, representing ten.

The number system of the Romans was awkward compared to the Arabic system we use today. As Roman numerals grew larger, they became increasingly hard to read. Since the Romans had no zero, arithmetic calculation was difficult. Although no longer used in mathematics, Roman numerals

Dum petit in terrā Siculā Proserpina flōrēs,
    errat ab ancillīs saepe puella suīs;
nam, "Prope nōn flōs est pulcherrimus," inquit, "amīcae.
    Saepe in dēsertōs īre necesse locōs."
Sōla ōlim sōlīs in agrīs dēfessa puella   5
    (heu!) sedet, et flōrem multum habet atque bonum,
cum prope sub parvā magnum videt arbore flōrem
    et petit. At flōrem nōn superāre potest.
Tum magis atque magis Proserpina parva labōrat
    strēnua—sed frūstrā! Flōs magis haeret ibi.   10
Ecce! Puella, cavē! Mōnstrum est! Temerāria, mōnstrum
    (esque sine ancillīs sōla), puella, cavē!
At subitō parvā est discissa sub arbore terra,
    appārent ātrī quattuor intus equī.
"Ancillae, ferte auxilium!" Proserpina clāmat,   15
    "Māter," et "auxilium fer, dea magna, mihi!
Dīs mē habet!" At cēlat lacrimantem terra puellam.
    Invenit et dominam servula nūlla suam.

terra, -ae (*f*), land, earth, ground	**magis,** more
Siculus, -a, -um, Sicilian	**mōnstrum, -ī** (*n*), warning
flōs, flōris (*m*), flower	**-que,** and
prope, near by	**sine** (+ *abl.*), without
pulcherrimus, -a, -um, loveliest	**est discissa,** was torn apart,
locus, -ī (*m*), place	opened up
ōlim, one day	**āter, ātra, ātrum,** black
heu, alas	**intus,** inside (the opening)
multus, -a, -um, much, in abundance	**dea, -ae** (*f*), goddess
atque, and	**Dīs, Dītis** (*m*), Dis, the god of the
parvus, -a, -um, small	underworld
at, but	**servula, -ae** (*f*), slave-girl
superō, superāre (1), to overcome,	
to pull up	

9 Phaëthon
(after Chapter 16)

Phaëthon was really the Sun-god's son, but none of his friends would believe him when he boasted about it. In fact, he began to doubt it himself. So one day he journeyed far to the east to the palace of the Sun-god, the stately golden fortress from which every morning he begins his journey through the skies. The god laughed when he heard of his son's doubts and distress and said, "To prove to you beyond doubt that I am your father, ask anything at all of me and I promise you on my unbreakable word that I will grant it." Phaëthon asked to be allowed for one day to drive the great sun-chariot with its four huge horses.

There was nothing the Sun-god was less willing to grant. He looked at Phaëthon and at the great horses and knew that the boy would not be able to control them. But he had given his word, and the youth set off to his certain death. The horses got the bit between their teeth and came so near the earth with their blazing chariot that Jupiter, king of gods and men, had no choice but to destroy them with his thunderbolts to save the earth and everyone on it from being destroyed by fire.

Sūmit ab invītō genitōre ēlātus habēnās
    - et puer immēnsōs incitat ācer equōs.
Mox procul ā summō timidus videt aethere terrās,
    tum dextrā sociīs (ēn!) equus hinnit equīs.
Et, "Sociī, nōn est onus hoc solitum," inquit. "Habēnās   5
    quae tenet hās hodiē, nōnne remissa manus?
Est aurīga puer! Puer hōrum at nūllus equōrum
    est dominus. Retinet nōn mea colla puer!
Noster abest dominus. Nunc lūdere tempus, amīcī,
    nunc dēvertere iter. Quō placet īre licet."   10
Currus deinde patris vestīgia certa relinquit.
    Dēscendit, Phaëthon nec retinēre potest.
Incipit et iam vīcīnōs nimis ūrere montēs;
    vīcīnōs currus iam nimis ūrit agrōs.
Mox urbēs nūllae incolumēs; mox oppida nūlla,   15
    nūlla propinquantēs nōn timet aula rotās.
Iuppiter illa videt; quī, "Nōn placet," inquit, "equōrum
    sī terrās omnēs ūrere turba potest.
Ō Cyclōpes, ubī sunt fulmina?" Fulmina mittit.
    Servat sīc terrās. Heu! Phaëthonta necat.   20

sūmō, sūmere (3), to take
invītus, -a, -um, unwilling
genitor, genitōris (m), father
ēlātus, -a, -um, delighted
habēnae, -ārum (f pl), reins
ācer, ācris, ācre, eager
ā summō . . . aethere, from the
    heights of heaven
terra, -ae (f), land
dextrā, on the right
sociīs . . . equīs, to the horses
    accompanying (him)
ēn, look, behold
hinniō, hinnīre (4), to whinny
socius, -ī (m), companion
hoc, this
solitus, -a, -um, usual
hās, these
nōnne remissa manus? is it not a
    feeble hand?
hōrum, of these
at, but
retineō, retinēre (2), to hold
    back, restrain
colla, -ōrum (n pl), neck
lūdō, lūdere (3), to play

quō placet īre licet, we may go
    where we please
currus, chariot
certus, -a, -um, fixed, usual
relinquō, relinquere (3), to leave
nec, and not
incipiō, incipere (3), to begin
nimis, too, too much
ūrō, ūrere (3), to burn
mōns, montis (m), mountain
oppidum, -ī (n), town
propinquantēs, approaching
aula, -ae (f), hall, palace
Iuppiter, Iovis (m), Jupiter
illa, those things, that
nōn placet, I don't like it
turba, -ae (f), crowd
Cyclōpes, Cyclōpum (m pl), Cyclopes
    (giants who manufactured
    thunderbolts for Jupiter)
fulmen, fulminis (n), thunderbolt
servō, servāre (1), to save
sīc, in this way
Heu! Alas!
Phaëthonta, Phaëthon (acc. case)
necō, necāre (1), to kill

95

PRONUNCIATION

The pronunciation of Latin is best learned by imitation of the teacher. Most consonants are pronounced as in English, but the following should be noted:

b before s or t is pronounced as English *p*: **urbs.**
c is always hard and pronounced as English *k*: **cibus.**
g is hard, as in English "get": **gemit.**
gn in the middle of a word may be pronounced as the *ngn* in English "hangnail": **magnus.**
i before a vowel is a consonant and pronounced as English *y*: **iānua.**
r should be rolled: **rāmus.**
s is pronounced as in English "sing," never as in "roses": **cīvis.**
v is pronounced as English *w*: **vīlla.**

The following approximations are offered for the pronunciation of short and long vowels. In addition, long vowels should be held for a longer time than short ones.

SHORT	LONG
a = English "alike" (**pater**)	ā = English "father" (**māter**)
e = English "pet" (**ego**)	ē = English "date" (**dēscendō**)
i = English "sip" (**iterum**)	ī = English "sleep" (**īrātus**)
o = English "for" (**omnēs**)	ō = English "holy" (**in hortō**)
u = English "foot" (**ubi**)	ū = English "boot" (**ūnus**)

The diphthong **ae** is pronounced as the *y* in English "sky" (**amīcae**). The diphthong **au** is pronounced as the *ow* in English "how" (**audit**). The diphthong **ei** is pronounced as the "ay" in English "say" (**deinde**).

Latin words are accented according to simple rules. If the next to the last syllable has a long vowel or a diphthong, it will receive the accent:

discḗdō

If the next to the last syllable has a short vowel followed by two consonants, it will usually receive the accent:

exténdō

Otherwise, the accent falls on the third syllable from the end:

Británnicus

Careful observation of the long marks (macrons) over the vowels will thus help with both pronunciation and accenting of Latin words.

FORMS

The following charts show the forms of typical Latin nouns, adjectives, and verbs in the cases and tenses presented in this book. As an aid in pronunciation, markings of long vowels and of accents are included.

I. Nouns

Number / Case	1st Declension Fem.	2nd Declension Masc.	2nd Declension Masc.	2nd Declension Neut.	3rd Declension Masc.	3rd Declension Fem.	3rd Declension Neut.
Singular							
Nominative	puélla	sérvus	púer	báculum	páter	vōx	nómen
Genitive	puéllae	sérvī	púerī	báculī	pátris	vōcis	nóminis
Accusative	puéllam	sérvum	púerum	báculum	pátrem	vōcem	nómen
Ablative	puéllā	sérvō	púerō	báculō	pátre	vōce	nómine
Plural							
Nominative	puéllae	sérvī	púerī	bácula	pátrēs	vōcēs	nómina
Genitive	puellárum	servórum	puerórum	baculórum	pátrum	vōcum	nóminum
Accusative	puéllās	sérvōs	púerōs	bácula	pátrēs	vōcēs	nómina
Ablative	puéllīs	sérvīs	púerīs	báculīs	pátribus	vōcibus	nomínibus

97

II. Adjectives

Number Case	1st and 2nd Declension			3rd Declension		
	Masc.	*Fem.*	*Neut.*	*Masc.*	*Fem.*	*Neut.*
Singular						
Nominative	mágnus	mágna	mágnum	ómnis	ómnis	ómne
Genitive	mágnī	mágnae	mágnī	ómnis	ómnis	ómnis
Accusative	mágnum	mágnam	mágnum	ómnem	ómnem	ómne
Ablative	mágnō	mágnā	mágnō	ómnī	ómnī	ómnī
Plural						
Nominative	mágnī	mágnae	mágna	ómnēs	ómnēs	ómnia
Genitive	magnórum	magnárum	magnórum	ómnium	ómnium	ómnium
Accusative	mágnōs	mágnās	mágna	ómnēs	ómnēs	ómnia
Ablative	mágnīs	mágnīs	mágnīs	ómnibus	ómnibus	ómnibus

III. Numbers

Case	Masc.	Fem.	Neut.	Masc.	Fem.	Neut.	Masc.	Fem.	Neut.
Nominative	únus	úna	únum	dúo	dúae	dúo	trēs	trēs	tría
Genitive	úníus	úníus	úníus	duórum	duárum	duórum	tríum	tríum	tríum
Accusative	únum	únam	únum	dúōs	dúās	dúo	trēs	trēs	tría
Ablative	únō	únā	únō	duóbus	duábus	duóbus	tríbus	tríbus	tríbus

IV. Regular Verbs

The Present Tense

Number and Person		1st Conjugation	2nd Conjugation	3rd Conjugation		4th Conjugation
	Infinitive	paráre	habére	míttere	iácere (-iō)	audíre
	Imperative	párā	hábē	mítte	iáce	aúdī
		paráte	habéte	míttite	iácite	audíte
Singular	1	párō	hábeō	míttō	iáciō	aúdiō
	2	párās	hábēs	míttis	iácis	aúdis
	3	párat	hábet	míttit	iácit	aúdit
Plural	1	parámus	habémus	míttimus	iácimus	audímus
	2	parátis	habétis	míttitis	iácitis	audítis
	3	párant	hábent	míttunt	iáciunt	aúdiunt

The Imperfect Tense

Number and Person		1st Conjugation	2nd Conjugation	3rd Conjugation		4th Conjugation
Singular	1	parábam	habébam	mittébam	iaciébam	audiébam
	2	parábās	habébās	mittébās	iaciébās	audiébās
	3	parábat	habébat	mittébat	iaciébat	audiébat
Plural	1	parābámus	habēbámus	mittēbámus	iaciēbámus	audiēbámus
	2	parābátis	habēbátis	mittēbátis	iaciēbátis	audiēbátis
	3	parábant	habébant	mittébant	iaciébant	audiébant

V. Irregular Verbs

The Present Tense

Number and Person		Infinitive	ésse	pósse	vélle	nólle	íre	férre
Singular	1		sum	póssum	vólō	nólō	éō	férō
	2		es	pótes	vīs	nōn vīs	īs	fers
	3		est	pótest	vult	nōn vult	it	fert
Plural	1		súmus	póssumus	vólumus	nólumus	ímus	férimus
	2		éstis	potéstis	vúltis	nōn vúltis	ítis	fértis
	3		sunt	póssunt	vólunt	nólunt	éunt	férunt

The Imperfect Tense

Number and Person		éram	póteram	volébam	nōlébam	íbam	ferébam
Singular	1	éram	póteram	volébam	nōlébam	íbam	ferébam
	2	érās	póterās	volébās	nōlébās	íbās	ferébās
	3	érat	póterat	volébat	nōlébat	íbat	ferébat
Plural	1	erámus	poterámus	volēbámus	nōlēbámus	ibámus	ferēbámus
	2	erátis	poterátis	volēbátis	nōlēbátis	ibátis	ferēbátis
	3	érant	póterant	volébant	nōlébant	íbant	ferébant

Note: The imperatives of **nōlle** are **nōlī** (*sing.*) and **nōlīte** (*pl.*).

101

Vocabulary*

A

13	ā or ab (+ *abl.*)	from
3	ábeō, abíre (*irreg.*)	to go away
11	ábsum, abésse (*irreg.*)	to be away, absent
14	áccidit, accídere (3)	to happen
2	ad (+ *acc.*)	to, towards, at, near
5	adhúc	still
6	advéniō, adveníre (4)	to reach, arrive at
16	advesperáscit, advesperáscere (3)	to get dark
16	aedifícium, -ī (*n*)	building
1	aestáte	in summer
8	Áge! Ágite!	Come on!
2	áger, ágrī (*m*)	field
14	ágō, ágere (3)	to do, drive
15	álius, ália, áliud	another, other
9	áliī . . . áliī . . .	some . . . others . . .
1	álter, áltera, álterum	the other, a second
2	ámbulō, ambuláre (1)	to walk
2	amíca, -ae (*f*)	friend
3	amícus, -ī (*m*)	friend
4	ámō, amáre (1)	to like, love
10	ancílla, -ae (*f*)	slave-woman
15	appáreō, appārére (2)	to appear
4	appropínquō, appropinquáre (1)	to approach
1	árbor, árboris (*f*)	tree
11	área, -ae (*f*)	open space, threshing-floor
6	arrípiō, arrípere (3)	to grab hold of, snatch
14	ars, ártis (*f*)	skill
4	ascéndō, ascéndere (3)	to climb, go up, climb into (a carriage)
4	aúdiō, audíre (4)	to hear, listen to
13	auríga, -ae (*m*)	charioteer
6	auxílium, -ī (*n*)	help

B

10	báculum, -ī (*n*)	stick
12	bónus, -a, -um	good
15	bōs, bóvis (*m/f*)	ox, cow
2	brévī témpore	in a short time, soon
8	Británnia, -ae (*f*)	Britain
3	Británnicus, -a, -um	British

*Numbers at the left refer to the chapter in which the word first appears.

C

3	cádō, cádere (3)	to fall
16	caélum, -ī (n)	sky
6	cálidus, -a, -um	warm
12	cánis, cánis (m/f)	dog
1	cántō, cantáre (1)	to sing
16	caúpō, caupṓnis (m)	innkeeper
16	caupṓna, -ae (f)	inn
4	Cávē! Cavḗte!	Be careful!
8	celériter	quickly
14	celérrimē	very fast, quickly
11	cḗlō, cēláre (1)	to hide
15	céntum	a hundred
14	céssō, cessáre (1)	to be idle, do nothing
11	cíbus, -ī (m)	food
14	císium, -ī (n)	light two-wheeled carriage
10	císta, -ae (f)	trunk, chest, box
13	cívis, cívis (m)	citizen
3	clámō, clāmáre (1)	to shout
5	clámor, clāmóris (m)	shout, shouting
14	commótus, -a, -um	moved
9	compléxū	in an embrace
14	cóncidō, concídere (3)	to fall down
4	cōnspíciō, cōnspícere (3)	to catch sight of
7	cónsulō, cōnsúlere (3)	to consult
12	cónvocō, convocáre (1)	to call together
10	crās	tomorrow
8	cubículum, -ī (n)	room, bedroom
14	Cúius . . . ?	Whose . . . ?
14	cúlpa, -ae (f)	fault, blame
12	cum (+ abl.)	with
14	cúnctī, -ae, -a	all
1	Cūr . . . ?	Why . . . ?
10	cū́rō, cūráre (1)	to look after, attend to
2	cúrrō, cúrrere (3)	to run
16	custódiō, custōdī́re (4)	to guard

D

15	décem	ten
16	décimus, -a, -um	tenth
2	dēféssus, -a, -um	tired
8	deínde	then, next
4	dēscéndō, dēscéndere (3)	to come or go down, climb down
14	dēvértō, dēvértere (3)	to turn aside
6	díēs, diḗī (m)	day

103

9	discédō, discédere (3)	to go away, depart
15	díū	for a long time
16	dómina, -ae (f)	mistress, lady of the house
11	dóminus, -ī (m)	master
4	dórmiō, dormíre (4)	to sleep
7	dúcō, dúcere (3)	to lead, take, bring
1	dum	while, as long as
15	dúo, dúae, dúo	two

E

2	ē or ex (+ abl.)	from, out of
9	éam	her, it
10	éās	them
1	Écce!	Look! Look at . . . !
11	effúgiō, effúgere (3)	to run away, escape
5	égo	I
7	Éheu!	Alas!
2	éius	his, her, its
13	éō, íre (irreg.)	to go
10	éō ípsō témpore	at that very moment
6	éōs	them
7	epístula, -ae (f)	letter
10	équus, -ī (m)	horse
13	érat	(he, she, it) was
6	érrō, erráre (1)	to wander
	ésse (see sum)	
2	et	and
1	étiam	also
7	Eúgepae!	Hurray!
3	éum	him, it
2	ex or ē (+ abl.)	from, out of
6	excípiō, excípere (3)	to welcome
8	éxcitō, excitáre (1)	to rouse, wake (someone) up
10	exclámō, exclāmáre (1)	to exclaim, shout out
3	éxeō, exíre (irreg.)	to go out
15	exspéctō, exspectáre (1)	to look out for, wait for
14	éxtrahō, extráhere (3)	to drag out

F

1	fáciō, fácere (3)	to make, do
13	fátuus, -a, -um	stupid
6	férō, férre (irreg.)	to bring, carry
13	feróciter	fiercely
6	Férte auxílium!	Bring help! Help!
9	festínō, festīnáre (1)	to hurry
11	fília, -ae (f)	daughter

11	fílius, -ī (*m*)	son
15	fortásse	perhaps
12	fóssa, -ae (*f*)	ditch
4	frágor, fragóris (*m*)	crash, noise, din
11	fráter, frátris (*m*)	brother
6	frígidus, -a, -um	cool, cold
12	frōns, fróntis (*f*)	forehead
14	frústrā	in vain
3	fúrtim	stealthily

G

14	gaúdeō, gaudére (2)	to be glad, rejoice
3	gémō, gémere (3)	to groan
10	gérō, gérere (3)	to wear
16	Graécus, -a, -um	Greek

H

10	hábeō, habére (2)	to have, hold
1	hábitō, habitáre (1)	to live, dwell
14	haéreō, haerére (2)	to stick
9	hīc (*adverb*)	here
2	hódiē	today
9	hóra, -ae (*f*)	hour
3	hórtus, -ī (*m*)	garden

I

10	iáciō, iácere (3)	to throw
1	iam	now, already
9	iánitor, iānitóris (m)	doorkeeper
9	iánua, -ae (*f*)	door
5	íbi	there
11	id quod	that which, what
3	ídem, éadem, ídem	the same
13	idéntidem	again and again
4	ígitur	therefore
6	ignávus, -a, -um	cowardly, lazy
11	ílle, ílla, íllud	that, he, she, it
12	immóbilis, -is, -e	motionless
11	impédiō, impedíre (4)	to hinder, prevent
1	in (+ *abl.*)	in, on
3	in (+ *acc.*)	into
10	íncitō, incitáre (1)	to spur on, urge on
14	incólumis, -is, -e	unhurt, safe and sound
8	índuō, indúere (3)	to put on
4	īnfírmus,ʾ -a, -um	weak, shaky
7	ínquit	(he, she) says, said
10	intéreā	meanwhile

14	interpéllō, interpelláre (1)	to interrupt
8	íntrō, intráre (1)	to enter, go in
12	inúrō, inúrere (3)	to brand
12	invéniō, veníre (4)	to come upon, find
10	ípse, ípsa, ípsum	-self, very
11	íra, -ae (f)	anger
14	írā commótus	made angry, in a rage
3	īrátus, -a, -um	angry
	íre (see éō)	
3	Íta vérō!	Yes!
1	Itália, -ae (f)	Italy
16	ítaque	and so, therefore
13	íter, itíneris (n)	journey
13	íter fácere	to travel
8	íterum	again, a second time
10	iúbeō, iubére (2)	to order

L

3	labốrō, labōráre (1)	to work
9	lácrimō, lacrimáre (1)	to weep, cry
1	laétus, -a, -um	happy, glad
12	látrō, lātráre (1)	to bark
7	légō, légere (3)	to read
2	léntē	slowly
11	líberī, -ốrum (m pl)	children
12	líttera, -ae (f)	letter (of the alphabet)
15	lóngus, -a, -um	long
8	lúcet, lūcére (2)	to be light, to be day
6	lúpus, -ī (m)	wolf

M

3	mádidus, -a, -um	dripping, soaked, wet
4	mágnus, -a, -um	big, great, large, loud (voice, laugh)
5	mấne	early in the day, in the morning
9	máneō, manére (2)	to remain, stay
8	mắter, mắtris (f)	mother
4	mē	me
9	mḗcum	with me
7	méus, -a, -um	my
8	míhi	for me, to me
15	mílle	a thousand
3	Mínimē!	No!
9	míser, mísera, míserum	unhappy, miserable
9	míttō, míttere (3)	to send
4	moléstus, -a, -um	troublesome, annoying
3	moléstus, -ī (m)	pest

106

14	móveō, movére (2)	to move
12	mox	soon, presently
3	múltī, -ae, -a	many
15	múrmur, múrmuris (n)	murmur, rumble
11	mússō, mussáre (1)	to mutter

N

8	nam	for
8	nārrátor, nārrātóris (m)	narrator
9	nátō, natáre (1)	to swim
3	-ne	(indicates a question)
15	Neápolis	Naples
7	necésse	necessary
9	némō	no one
6	néque . . . néque . . .	neither . . . nor . . .
9	nésciō, nescíre (4)	to be ignorant, not know
3	níhil	nothing
9	nóbīs	for us
12	nócte	at night
6	nólō, nólle (irreg.)	to be unwilling, not wish
1	nómen, nóminis (n)	name
1	nómine	by name, called
2	nōn	not
8	nóndum	not yet
8	nōs	we, us
14	nóster, nóstra, nóstrum	our
15	nóvem	nine
11	nox, nóctis (f)	night
9	núllus, -a, -um	no
11	númerus, -ī (m)	number
11	nunc	now
7	núntius, -ī (m)	messenger

O

14	obsérvō, observáre (1)	to watch
5	occupátus, -a, -um	busy
15	óctō	eight
12	olfáciō, olfácere (3)	to catch the scent of, smell
14	olīvétum, -ī (n)	olive grove
8	ómnēs, ómnia	all, everyone, everything
15	ónus, óneris (n)	load, burden

P

10	parátus, -a, -um	ready, prepared
11	párēns, paréntis (m/f)	parent
6	párō, paráre (1)	to prepare, get ready
13	párs, pártis (f)	part

107

5	páter, pátris (m)	father
9	per (+ acc.)	through, along
16	perīculósus, -a, -um	dangerous
14	perículum, -ī (n)	danger
16	pernóctō, pernoctáre (1)	to spend the night
6	pertérritus, -a, -um	frightened, terrified
13	pēs, pédis (m)	foot
5	pétō, pétere (3)	to look for, seek, aim at, attack
1	pictúra, -ae (f)	picture
3	piscína, -ae (f)	fishpond
14	plácidē	gently, peacefully
15	plaústrum, -ī (n)	wagon, cart
11	plḗnus, -a, -um	full
10	pónō, pónere (3)	to put, place
11	pórta, -ae (f)	gate
10	pórtō, portáre (1)	to carry
6	póssum, pósse (irreg.)	to be able
13	póterat	(he, she) was able
13	praeclárus, -a, -um	distinguished, famous
15	praetéreā	besides, too, moreover
15	praetéreō, praeteríre (irreg.)	to go past
10	praetéxta (tóga)	with purple edge
7	prínceps, príncipis (m)	emperor
15	prócul	in the distance, far off
9	prōmíttō, prōmíttere (3)	to promise
6	própe (+ acc.)	near
1	puélla, -ae (f)	girl
3	púer, púerī (m)	boy

Q	1	quae	who
	4	Quális . . . ?	What sort of . . . ?
	13	Quam . . . !	How . . . !
	11	quámquam	although
	15	quáttuor	four
	6	Quem . . . ?	Whom . . . ?
	1	quī, quae, quod	who, which
	10	quídam, quaédam, quóddam	a certain
	1	Quid fácit . . . ?	What does . . . do?
	13	quiéscō, quiéscere (3)	to rest, keep quiet
	15	quīngéntī, -ae, -a	five hundred
	15	quīnquāgíntā	fifty
	15	quínque	five
	1	Quis . . . ? Quid . . . ?	Who . . . ? What . . . ?
	4	Quō . . . ?	Where . . . to?

1	quod	because, which
13	Quō īnstruméntō . . . ?	With what implement . . . ?
		How . . . ?
14	Quómodo . . . ?	In what way . . . ? How . . . ?
2	quóque	also
7	Quōs . . . ?	Whom . . . ?
15	Quot . . . ?	How many . . . ?

R

10	ráeda, -ae (f)	traveling carriage, coach
10	raedárius, -ī (m)	coachman
4	rámus, -ī (m)	branch
5	rédeō, redíre (irreg.)	to return
6	repéllō, repéllere (3)	to drive off, drive back
12	reprehéndō, reprehéndere (3)	to blame, scold
5	respóndeō, respondére (2)	to reply
7	révocō, revocáre (1)	to recall, call back
3	rídeō, rīdére (2)	to laugh, smile
13	(mágnō) rísū	with a loud laugh
6	rívus, -ī (m)	stream
12	rógō, rogáre (1)	to ask
7	Róma, -ae (f)	Rome
1	Rōmánus, -a, -um	Roman
15	róta, -ae (f)	wheel
1	rústicus, -a, -um	rustic, country-style
13	rústicus, -ī (m)	peasant

S

2	saépe	often
7	salútō, salūtáre (1)	to greet, welcome
7	Sálvē! Salvéte!	Greetings! Good morning! Hello!
3	sálvus, -a, -um	undamaged, all right, safe
10	sceléstus, -a, -um	wicked
7	scríbo, scríbere (3)	to write
11	sē	himself, herself, itself, themselves
9	secúndus, -a, -um	second
2	sed	but
1	sédeō, sedére (2)	to sit
9	sēmisómnus, -a, -um	half-asleep
4	sémper	always
7	senátor, senātóris (m)	senator
15	séptem	seven
13	séptimus, -a, -um	seventh
3	sérvus, -ī (m)	slave
15	sex	six

109

5	sī	if
15	siléntium, -ī (n)	silence
6	sílva, -ae (f)	woods, forest
9	símul	together, at the same time
10	sóleō, solére (2)	to be accustomed, in the habit of
3	sollícitus, -a, -um	anxious, worried
3	sólus, -a, -um	alone
11	sóror, soróris (f)	sister
3	spéctō, spectáre (1)	to watch, look at
5	státim	immediately
3	státua, -ae (f)	statue
10	stō, stáre (1)	to stand
10	stóla, -ae (f)	stola, a woman's outer-garment
8	strḗnuē	strenuously, hard
2	strḗnuus, -a, -um	active, energetic
1	sub (+ abl.)	under, beneath
3	súbitō	suddenly
1	sum, ésse (irreg.)	to be
8	súrgō, súrgere (3)	to get up, rise
9	súus, -a, -um	his, her, its, their (own)

T

13	tabellárius, -ī (m)	courier
9	táceō, tacére (2)	to be quiet
9	tácitē	silently
12	támen	however
2	tándem	at last
15	tántum	only
15	tárdus, -a, -um	slow
	tē (see tū)	
6	temerárius, -a, -um	rash, reckless, bold
9	témptō, temptáre (1)	to try
2	témpus, témporis (n)	time
9	téneō, tenére (2)	to hold
4	térreō, terrére (2)	to frighten, terrify
6	tímeō, timére (2)	to fear, be afraid of
5	tímidus, -a, -um	afraid
10	tóga, -ae (f)	toga
7	trádo, trádere (3)	to hand over
12	tráhō, tráhere (3)	to drag, pull
12	trēs, trēs, tría	three
4	tū (acc. tē)	you (sing.)
4	tum	at that moment, then
8	túnica, -ae (f)	tunic
5	túus, -a, -um	your

U 5 Úbi . . . ?   Where . . . ?
     1 úbi   where, when
    15 únus, -a, -um   one
     7 urbs, úrbis (f)   city
    11 úxor, uxóris (f)   wife

V 9 Válē! Valéte!   Goodbye!
    13 vehículum, -ī (n)   vehicle
        vélle (see vólō)
     5 véniō, venīre (4)   to come
    11 vérberō, verberáre (1)   to beat
    12 vestígium, -ī (n)   track, footprint, trace
     3 véxō, vexáre (1)   to annoy
    10 vía, -ae (f)   road, street
    16 viátor, viātóris (m)   traveler
     1 vīcínus, -a, -um   neighboring
     4 vídeō, vidére (2)   to see
    11 vílicus, -ī (m)   overseer, farm manager
     1 vílla, -ae (f)   farmhouse
     1 vílla rústica   farmhouse
    12 vínea, -ae (f)   vineyard
     3 vir, vírī (m)   man
    13 vírga, -ae (f)   stick
    16 vīs (from vólō)   you want
    15 vīs púlveris   cloud of dust
    13 vítō, vītáre (1)   to avoid
     6 vólō, vélle (irreg.)   to wish, want, be willing
     8 vōs   you (pl.)
     4 vōx, vócis (f)   voice
     6 vult (from vólō)   (he, she) wishes, wants